A MESSAGE TO THE
Glorious Church

VOLUME II

A Verse by Verse Study of
Ephesians Chapters 5-6

RICK JOYNER

MorningStar Publications
A DIVISION OF MORNINGSTAR FELLOWSHIP CHURCH
P.O. Box 440
Wilkesboro, NC 28697

A Message to the Glorious Church, Volume II
Rick Joyner
Copyright © 2003

All rights reserved.

International Standard Book Number—1-929371-30-6

All Scripture quotations are taken from the New American Standard Version unless otherwise indicated, copyright (c) 1983 by Thomas Nelson, Inc.

Table of Contents

Preface

This is a verse by verse study of Ephesians, Chapters Five and Six. Even though this is Volume II of the study, it can be read and understood without having read Volume I, since these two chapters have a message that is both powerful and unique on their own. The first four chapters of Ephesians give a sweeping but detailed vision of what the church is called to be, and the last two chapters impart practical wisdom about how to get us there.

As stated in my preface to Volume I, even though this is a verse by verse study of Ephesians, I do not consider it to be an in-depth study. There are numerous, individual verses in this Epistle which are worthy of having a whole book dedicated to them. In fact, there may be no other book in the Bible which has had so many books derived from its contents. It is truly worthy of this kind of attention. One could spend a lifetime studying the book of Ephesians and never exhaust its revelation. It is a universe in itself, ever expanding, reaching both deeper and higher at the same time. Therefore, my primary prayer as you read this book is that it stirs a continued, deeper study of this great treasure. I also pray that the Holy Spirit will use this study to grip your soul with devotion to become a part of the glorious church that we are called to be.

There will come a time when all that Paul describes in Ephesians will come to pass. Many other prophecies in both the Old and New Testaments corroborate this vision. So many other prophecies are now coming to pass it seems obvious that it is time to see the prophecies of the glorious bride of Christ also being fulfilled. There is a prophetic voice rising again that seems especially sent to prepare the bride for her coming King. Those who are hearing it are being stirred to make themselves ready.

As a pastor, I have had the privilege of observing a number of brides as they approach their wedding day. A bride's focus grows dramatically as the day gets closer and the activity gets more and more intense. On the wedding day, it all culminates. All the attention to the wedding itself is secondary since the primary concentration becomes making the bride as beautiful as she can possibly be. All over the world this same kind of activity seems to be growing in the church. The voice proclaiming that the Bridegroom is coming is getting louder and louder, but the greatest sign of all is the devotion of the bride to make herself ready for her King. This will culminate in a time of such intense activity and focus that it will be hard for anyone to be close who is not likewise focused on this ultimate purpose.

Ephesians is about the glorious calling and purpose of the church, but it goes without saying that the main point is that our King is deserving of a bride like no other. This is a greater story than any fairy tale could ever be—and it is absolutely real! You are called to be a part of it, as fantastic as it may seem. And you will live happily ever after. What could we possibly do with our lives that is more important than this? What is worthy of more of our attention and devotion than being the bride we are called to be for Him?

This is the cry of the prophets, and the two chapters of Ephesians which we are going to study in this volume. Our goal should be to gain knowledge of the Lord's ways and our calling, but we must not stop there. We must go on to turn this knowledge into a heart devotion that does not stop preparing for Him until the day our King appears and the feast begins.

Someone is going to walk in everything that Paul saw the glorious church becoming. Why not you? Ultimately our success in this life will not be measured in the blessings we have received, or even what we have done, but what we have become, and the blessing we have become to Him.

PART VI

Growing in the Power, Authority, and Character of Christ

A Study of Ephesians
Chapter 5

CHAPTER ONE

Imitators of God

O ur text for this chapter is Ephesians 5:1-2:

Therefore be imitators of God, as beloved children;

and walk in love, just as Christ also loved you, and gave Himself up for us, an offering and a sacrifice to God as a fragrant aroma.

The mere thought that we can be imitators of God is so remarkable that it seems like the ultimate presumption. However, this is what we are commanded to do! The most sobering truth is that we are all called to be like the Lord and to do the works He did! This is our most basic purpose for being on the earth—to represent Him by being like Him and doing His works.

Of course there is no way we could ever accomplish this without Him, and that is the point. He has given us His Holy Spirit to manifest Himself through us. The power of the One who created the universe is living within us, and He will use us when we come into agreement with Him. This is our highest and most basic quest—to think His thoughts, to speak His words, to go through life seeing with His eyes, hearing with His ears, and understanding others with His heart. Growing in all of these things are some of the basic ways we can measure true Christian maturity.

Of course, a question now arises: "How do we do this?" He tells us how to begin in this same verse—to **"walk in love."** This is not a general "sloppy agape," but as the verse states, we are to love with the same kind of love the Lord loved us with. This is more than just having affection for others. The way He loved us was to give His life for us, and this is what we are called to do for others. He was an offering and a sacrifice, and we are called to be the same. We are here to live a life of sacrifice for others.

When we were redeemed, we were bought with a price and are no longer our own—we belong to Christ. He did not redeem us just so we could have better lives here, and then eternal life in heaven. These are benefits too wonderful to comprehend, but we were redeemed for more than that—we are called to be His representatives on the earth until He returns. Then we will rule with Him over the earth, a job for which we are now being prepared.

We may think that ruling over the earth will be "heaven," but it will be work even though we will have our "glorified bodies" and dwell in a heavenly realm with Him. The reason He rules over the earth for a thousand years is because it will take that long to restore the earth. This is the time that Peter referred to as **"the period of restoration of all things"** in Acts 3:21. Here we cannot get into much detail, but it is important that we have a vision for the **"restoration of all things."** As long as a single soul is still in bondage to the devil, our work is not done. We were not just redeemed for our own sakes, but to be part of God's plan for redeeming and restoring the earth from all of the consequences of the Fall.

This may all seem too remarkable to someone who has not been saturated with the exhortations of our callings in the Scriptures, but they are in fact the basic reason we remain on the earth after our redemption. This life is more than anything, simply "training for reigning." To be imitators of God may sound like the most extreme presumption, but man was actually created in God's image and this is a basic purpose for all of mankind. Man was created to represent the Lord and rule over the physical creation on earth. We are right now laying the groundwork for the kingdom age in which this will be done.

Because **"God is love" (John 4:8)** this is the fundamental devotion that we must have in our life—to be an imitator of God. As with any building, if the foundation is not properly laid, everything built upon it can be in jeopardy, so we must get the foundation of love right. Even so we must then build upon it with power. How could we ever be an imitator of the Almighty without power? This is why we are told in II Timothy 3:5 that we are to not associate with those who hold to a form of godliness but deny the power. The Lord wants His people to be known for their love, but He also wants the world to know that His love has power.

Many of the popular movies of our times have a basic theme of people using supernatural power, such as: *Star Wars, X-Men, The Matrix, Harry Potter,* and *The Lord of the Rings,* as well as a host of others. The reason is because men were created to have fellowship with God who is supernatural, and therefore, there is a deep yearning in men for the supernatural.

Even though this is mostly fantasy, kids are being captivated by the supernatural. They are drawn to any kind of hope of actually experiencing it, such as witchcraft and the dark arts. This is the tragic result of much of the church declaring that God does not do miracles anymore—something which He never stated anywhere in Scripture, but in fact declared the opposite. The Scriptures are very clear that the true Christian life is supernatural, filled with the power of the Holy Spirit. We are actually warned not to associate with those who hold to a form of godliness, but deny the power (see II Timothy 3:5).

As we get closer to the end of this age, those who do not know the true, supernatural power of God will become increasingly subject to the evil, supernatural power of the enemy. We are headed for a power confrontation like has never before been seen on the earth.

As we discussed earlier, what the Lord Jesus Himself promised is actually even better than anything Hollywood has yet been able to come up with. He said that if we just had faith as big as a mustard seed, we could command a mountain to be plucked up and cast into the sea. He did marvelous things like walking on water, and then told us if we believed in Him we could do the same things, and even greater things. Some are going to walk in this. Why not us? We are told to be imitators of God, and He actually wants us to do the works He did, and even greater ones, to testify that He indeed was sent from the Father.

C H A P T E R   T W O

Paths to Destruction

O ur text for this chapter is Ephesians 5:3:

But do not let immorality or any impurity or greed even be named among you, as is proper among saints.

Immorality is understood to be any form of sex outside of marriage. However, what many people fail to see is that **"impurity"** is usually listed alongside immorality. What is impurity? Basically impurity is anything that we would do with our bodies that we would not do in the presence of the Lord. As we are told in I Corinthians 6:18-20:

Flee immorality. Every other sin that a man commits is outside the body, but the immoral man sins against his own body.

Or do you not know that your body is a temple of the Holy Spirit who is in you, whom you have from God, and that you are not your own?

For you have been bought with a price: therefore glorify God in your body.

Our bodies are temples of the Holy Spirit and His first name defines His most basic character—He is holy! If we are going to be hosts to Him by providing our bodies as His temple, we too must be holy.

Now the very word "holy" is often perceived as a form of legalism. And it is true that many have turned to legalism in their attempt to be holy, and thereby seek to impose their form of holiness and legalism on others in a way which has done great damage to the actual meaning of the word "holy." However, true holiness is the way we were created, radiating dignity and carrying itself with such honor and respect that we are immediately attracted to it instead of repelled, as we are by legalism.

The Lord said one of the major signs of the last days would be, **"And because lawlessness is increased, most people's love will grow cold" (Matthew 24:12).** In Romans 6:19, we are told how this lawlessness begins in a person, **"For just as you presented your members as slaves to impurity and to lawlessness, resulting in further lawlessness..."** Impurity is one of the primary ways that lawlessness gets a grip on a person's soul, leading to further lawlessness.

If compromise occurs in this area, it will also occur in other areas until there is a grip of lawlessness—questioning all sound doctrine and every spiritual discipline. Love for God will have also grown cold. This is one of the major paths to the apostasy and falling away from the faith, which the Scriptures warn us about.

Lately, I have been shocked by reports from some youth leaders about a doctrine circulating among teenagers and young adults in which one can have oral sex and still remain a "technical virgin." I have been even more grieved after talking to professional athletes who quit going to church because the pastors were hitting on their wives. These pastors were justifying their actions by a doctrine, stating that because King David and Solomon were so anointed, they needed many wives and concubines. These pastors said they needed many also because they were "so anointed." This is a grievously widespread doctrine in some parts of the church now, causing many to fall into snares from which few recover. These are **"doctrines of demons" (I Timothy 4:1),** leading many to the lawlessness and apostasy that the Lord made clear is the very reason for the final judgment of God which will come upon the world.

Sex in the relationship of marriage is one of the truly wonderful gifts that God gave to mankind. Outside of marriage it is one of the more destructive sins, and leads to the perversion of soul—the very lawlessness that will bring the wrath of God upon the world. Galatians 5:19-21 makes this clear:

Now the deeds of the flesh are evident, which are: immorality, impurity, sensuality,

idolatry, sorcery, enmities, strife, jealousy, outbursts of anger, disputes, dissensions, factions,

***envying, drunkenness, carousing, and things like these, of which I forewarn you just as I have forewarned you that* those who practice such things shall not inherit the kingdom of God.**

Let me repeat that last sentence one more time—**"those who practice such things shall not inherit the kingdom of God."**

Now let us go back to the verse for this chapter and notice how **"greed"** is named right in with immorality and impurity. Greed in any form opens the door to the perversion of soul which is lust. Lust may be sexual or other things, such as lust for money, power, fame, etc. Lust is basic selfishness, and is the primary counter power to the love that we are called to have and live by. This is why all of these lead to our "love growing cold."

If any of these things have attached themselves to us, we should never try to justify them. This is what leads to deception and destruction. Never try to justify or rationalize away the clear Word of God. Flee from any leaders in the church who are prone to do this. If you have fallen to sin, repentance is the only path that can restore your life in God and keep you on the path of life. Turn to the cross, acknowledging your sins and begging for the grace that the Son of God will surely give to you. But do not fall to the delusion that His grace is the perpetual forgiveness for repeated sins. He will forgive us many times if we are indeed repenting, which is turning away from the sin and sincerely trying to walk uprightly. However, the Scriptures are clear that those who "practice unrighteousness" and "practice lawlessness" are headed for destruction, as Hebrews 10:29 makes clear:

> **How much severer punishment do you think he will deserve who has trampled under foot the Son of God, and has regarded as unclean the blood of the covenant by which he was sanctified, and has insulted the Spirit of grace?**

As we are told in Galatians 5:13-14, **"For you were called to freedom, brethren; only do not turn your freedom into an opportunity for the flesh, but through love serve one another. For the whole Law is fulfilled in one word, in the statement, You shall love your neighbor as yourself!"** The primary way we counter these deeds of the flesh is to walk in love. We give ourselves to loving the Lord and being a proper host to Him in His temple, our bodies. We give ourselves to loving one another and not doing anything that causes our brothers or sisters to stumble.

In the next verse, Ephesians 5:4, we are told:

> **and there must be no filthiness and silly talk, or coarse jesting, which are not fitting, but rather giving of thanks.**

Jesus Himself is called "the Word." He is the Communication from God. The Word of God has infinite value and power. Our words also have value and power to the degree that we have credibility and abide in the Lord. Therefore, we should treat words with the utmost care, which is the reason for the exhortation of this verse.

The Lord said in Matthew 12:34, **"For the mouth speaks out of that which fills the heart."** If filthiness and silliness are coming out of our mouths, it is because that is what is in our hearts. Filthiness and silly talk is like steam seeping from a teapot. If that steam were capped, the teapot would soon build up enough power to blow the kitchen up. However, because it is allowed to just seep out, it is just an irritating noise. Our words would have much more power if we likewise controlled their release.

The Lord also said, **"Not what enters into the mouth defiles the man, but what proceeds out of the mouth, this defiles the man" (Matthew 15:11).** We are defiling ourselves when we speak that which is filthy or coarse.

We are also told that there should be no **"coarse jesting" (Ephesians 5:4).** It should be noted this does not mean that there can be no jesting, just that it should not be "coarse." If you will allow a "thus saith Rick" here, high quality, mature, clean jesting can help the spiritual atmosphere of a church or ministry. Too many have been deceived by the religious spirit which implies that anything which is humorous or fun cannot be God. We must not forget that God commanded much more feasting than fasting. The Lord deeply mourns over the condition of mankind, but He also loves and has a very good time with His children. When we begin to take ourselves too seriously, it is usually the result of a stronghold of pride overtaking us. When humor departs, it is almost always the result of a religious spirit entering. However, it is important that jesting should not be filthy, silly, or coarse, which is below the dignity of the sons and daughters of the King.

We are also told in this verse that in place of these things which defile us, there should be the giving of thanks. Few seem to realize how powerful the giving of thanks can be. In fact, we are told in Psalm 100:4 that we **"enter His gates with thanksgiving, and His courts with praise."** Therefore, those who are thankful will enter the domain of the Lord, and as they learn to move higher into praise they will dwell in His very presence. Contrary to this, a complainer will fall further into darkness and the domain of the evil one, resulting in a whole lot more to complain about!

We should start every day by thanking the Lord for all of His blessings and goodness. There is a lot wrong in the world, in every church, and in every life, but faith will always see potential more than problems. If we are going to be aligned with the Lord, having a positive, thankful heart is fundamental. However, this does not imply that we are ignorant or blind to problems. It is simply knowing that God is much greater than any problem. In the midst of the most serious trials we can thank Him because **"...we know that God causes all things to work together for good to those who love God, to those who are called according to His purpose" (Romans 8:28).** Everything in our life is guaranteed by God to work out for our good. How could we not be in a state of continual thanksgiving?

So we see in these verses that Paul moves from warning about the consequences of immorality and impurity, to not even coarse jesting, **"but rather giving of thanks" (Ephesians 5:4).** Have you ever considered that the giving of thanks can help to keep us away from these evils? It does this by keeping us in the presence of the Lord, where these things are so obviously out of place and appalling when we see in the light of His glory.

CHAPTER THREE

Walking in Light

In our next verses, Ephesians 5:5-8, Paul continues with the theme that we addressed in the last chapter, but takes it a little further:

> **For this you know with certainty, that no immoral or impure person or covetous man, who is an idolater, has an inheritance in the kingdom of Christ and God.**
>
> **Let no one deceive you with empty words, for because of these things the wrath of God comes upon the sons of disobedience.**
>
> **Therefore do not be partakers with them;**
>
> **for you were formerly darkness, but now you are light in the Lord; walk as children of light...**

There have been many in every generation who try to deceive with **"empty words"** saying that God is love and, since He loves everyone, He will not exclude those who have such "problems" from the kingdom. **"Empty words"** are those which have their origin in man rather than the Word of God.

We can be absolutely sure that immorality, impurity, covetous, and idolatry will disqualify us from the kingdom of God. It is for these things that the wrath of God is coming upon the world, and if we are living by them we can count on His wrath coming

19

upon us as well. In fact, this is why His judgment begins with His own people, as we read in I Peter 4:17:

> **For it is time for judgment to begin with the household of God; and if it begins with us first, what will be the outcome for those who do not obey the gospel of God?**

I have a number of friends who have paid a high price for standing for biblical truth in relation to God's condemnation of things like homosexuality. It is interesting that such are usually branded "hate mongers" when in fact nothing could be further from the truth. No one loves homosexuals more than those who are willing to tell them the truth. If someone is headed for judgment and we do not warn them, how could we ever claim to love them? There may not be a people group that is more filled with hate and intolerance than the homosexual community, who demand tolerance and understanding from everyone else.

The truth is that God loves every homosexual, and it is because He loves them and everyone else, that His wrath is coming upon the earth against such things. However, it is hypocritical for us to rage against homosexuality if we are caught in immorality or even in "impurity," which will also disqualify us from the kingdom of God. The answer is not for the church to stop warning those who are practicing these things about the consequences, but for us to get free of the sin which so easily entangles us. Then we can warn from a position that is true and honest, and therefore endorsed by the Spirit of Truth, so as to bring conviction of sin.

We should also keep in mind that none of us are without sin, so none of us should be casting stones at others. Warnings should not be cast in such a way that they cause further injury such as stones do. We should be giving straightforward, biblically based warnings, which are also from the foundation of biblically required love, not hate, for those who are in bondage.

Christians should also be the first to stand up against gay bashing, or attacks against anyone for such things. These are sins for which one must be removed from the church if they are confronted with them according to the pattern given in Matthew 18 and refuse to repent. However, this is not done by casting stones or insults at them. If this biblical procedure is done with hate, or the "wrath of man," rather than the genuine sorrow we should have at the separation from a brother or sister who has fallen into the snare of the evil one, it will not be done righteously. As we are exhorted in James 1:19-20:

But let everyone be quick to hear, slow to speak and slow to anger; for the anger of man does not achieve the righteousness of God.

It is more than a cliché that we must love the sinner but hate the sin. We must love the sinner enough to tell them the truth of God's Word, not the humanistic philosophies that are rooted in the unsanctified mercy of the fallen human nature. Unsanctified mercy can be as damaging and as damning as the cruelty of self-righteousness.

Probably the greatest "prophet of judgment" in Scripture was Jeremiah. He did not stop warning people about the terrible tragedies which were sure to come as a result of their sins. Even so, neither did he stop weeping for the people, and begging God to show mercy on them. In fact, he did this so much that an entire book of the Bible resulted from it, the book of Lamentations.

Even after the conquering king offered Jeremiah a life of comfort and provision, Jeremiah elected to stay with the remnant of people left in Jerusalem, who would continue to reject him and his words, and ultimately kill him because he told them the truth. Given the choice, Jeremiah stayed with the ones who had caused him a lifetime of problems and because he loved them so much he just could not give up on them, until they killed him. Wasn't that Christlike? Can we maintain such a love in the face of the attacks and persecutions that we will surely receive from those who we likewise warn of the consequences of their sins? That is our calling.

If we are ever in the attitude where we hope God's judgment comes upon someone, then we are in the wrong spirit. Even

God does not want to send His judgments against sinners, and will do everything He can to not have to do this. When His judgment comes, it is simply the only resort left because it has become a cancer which will kill many others if not removed. Jeremiah wept for the people who had to suffer judgment because God was weeping too, and so will we if we are of His Spirit.

CHAPTER FOUR

Pleasing the Lord

Our verse for this chapter is Ephesians 5:10:
trying to learn what is pleasing to the Lord.

This simple statement encompasses the highest and most noble purpose of man. There is nothing we can ever do that will be more important, more powerful, more fruitful, and have a longer lasting impact on the world, than living our lives to please the Lord.

There is a reason we are called human "beings" rather than human "doings." Our highest calling is to be like Christ—not just do things for Him. Therefore our highest, most important devotion should be to be more like Him each day. What we become is more important than what we have done. How we would change if we measured the success of each day by how we had grown in our knowledge of Him, our obedience to Him, and how much more like Him we had become! Is there anything that should be measured above this in our lives?

The greatest human achievements are like the leaves on a tree. They may become brilliant for a little while in the fall, but then they fall to the earth and disappear. A few people may continue to hear about your achievements and be inspired by them, which is good, but just one moment of touching the heart of God Almighty is worth much more. Think about that one thing—you can touch God's heart today.

Many people spend their days contemplating how they can do something which will win them the recognition of someone they respect or love. Think about this—we can actually please the Creator of the Universe! We even have the ability to touch Him and move Him emotionally. What in this universe could be more important? If we get satisfaction out of pleasing our boss or spouse, it is good. How much more important will it be to hear on that great judgment day—**"Well done, good and faithful servant!" (Matthew 25:21 NKJV)**

I have heard athletes who received a gold medal at the Olympics say that they have had no experience which compares to standing on the podium, receiving their medal, and hearing their national anthem played. You can be sure that to hear God Almighty honor you on judgment day will be far better than any human honor could ever be.

What are the things that please the Lord? As stated, obviously the first is to be changed into the image of His Son. Jesus encompasses all of the things the Father loves. There is nothing in creation which has pleased Him more than His Son. So, the more we become like Christ, the more we will be pleasing to God.

In Colossians 1:9-10 we are also told, **"For this reason also, since the day we heard of it, we have not ceased to pray for you and to ask that you may be filled with the knowledge of His will in all spiritual wisdom and understanding, so that you may walk in a manner worthy of the Lord, to please Him in all respects..."** This sums up what should be the compelling drive of our lives—to be filled with the knowledge of His will, and to walk in a manner that pleases Him in all respects.

Such a devotion will also lead to the most fulfilling, satisfying, and fruitful life that we could ever live. We were known by Him and created in Christ Jesus before the foundation of the world. We are here with a specific purpose. The successful life is summed up in finding His will and doing it. In the end, that will be the true measure of greatness for everyone who ever lived on the earth, regardless of whatever else they may have accomplished.

So how do we find His will for our life? First we must be devoted to living and obeying the Word of God. The instructions in Paul's letters are filled with the answers to this question. Therefore, one who is truly in pursuit of a life that pleases God will have a passion for the Scriptures, always seeking to learn more about God, His ways, and what pleases Him. I have never known a truly godly person who was not also a devoted, daily, reader of the Scriptures.

A deep devotion to the written Word will be the foundation that every true servant of God is built upon. Then we must come to know His voice. As the Lord said concerning Himself being the Good Shepherd in John 10:4, **"When he puts forth all his own, he goes before them, and the sheep follow him because they know his voice."**

Some have said we no longer need the Lord to speak to us now since we have the written Word, but the written Word itself disputes this repeatedly. Knowing the Lord's voice is essential for a truly living relationship with Him. We are called to be the bride of Christ. How would any bride feel if on her wedding day her bridegroom came up to her and said, "Darling, I wrote this book for you so that I will never have to speak to you again." That would be a very sad wedding and marriage. The quality of any relationship will be determined by the quality of the communication, and we are betrothed to the greatest communicator ever—the living Word Himself!

Certainly the Bible is a treasure of immeasurable value, but it was never intended to supplant our living communication and relationship with the Lord. He does still speak to His people, and as John 10:4 implies, we will actually follow Him to the degree that we know His voice.

This is why we are told that **"Man shall not live on bread alone, but on every word that proceeds out of the mouth of God" (Matthew 4:4).** Note that this does not say we live by the words that "proceeded" from the mouth of God, past tense, but rather we live by the word that **"proceeds,"** present tense. It is good to know how God related to men, and it is good to remember the experiences that we have had with Him, but we do not live there—we live in the present. This is the basis of a life which pleases Him.

We are told in I Thessalonians 4:1: **"Finally then, brethren, we request and exhort you in the Lord Jesus, that, as you received from us instruction as to how you ought to walk and please God (just as you actually do walk), that you may excel still more."** This devotion to live and walk in a way that pleases the Lord should be the very basic devotion of our lives. In Hebrews 11:6 we are given further insight into what pleases the Lord:

> **"And without faith it is impossible to please Him, for he who comes to God must believe that He is, and that He is a rewarder of those who seek Him."**

So we know that faith pleases God. We should all therefore pursue growing in faith. To do this we must learn to live in a way that constantly pushes us beyond our comfort levels. This is in fact one of the most difficult things for most people to do. However, it is essential for us to grow in faith.

When the Lord used the metaphor comparing us to sheep, it was because in many ways people are like sheep. Most people are followers instead of leaders. Sheep are also some of the most timid animals. They are so timid that they will destroy a pasture, eating the grass down to the roots, rather than voluntarily moving to a greener pasture on their own. They resist change that much. So do people! This is one of the primary reasons why churches become so dry and lifeless; the people will resist change so much that it takes a pastor with supernatural strength, vision, and faith to keep them moving to new, greener pastures where there is life.

Such a willingness to press beyond the present into the new is a level of faith which in some ways may be greater than any other. In fact, as Dr. R.T. Kendall has noted in his great book, *Believing God,* it seems the only common denominator of those listed in Hebrews 11 as heroes of faith is that they all did something that no one had done before. It certainly takes great faith to press beyond the present limits of our time.

Hebrews 11:6 gives us the key to a life that is fresh and willing to move to green pastures—to come to God we must believe that He *IS,* not that He *WAS,* or *WILL BE,* but that He *IS!* This means that we must know Him in the present, not just in the past, or the future. Therefore, when we seek His will in the Scriptures, we are not just seeking to know the stories of how He related to men in the past, but the knowledge and inspiration to develop our own relationship with Him. We are not just seeking to hear the words of the Lord, but to hear the Word Himself.

C H A P T E R   F I V E

Being the Light

Now we will go on to the next verses in our study, Ephesians 5:11-12:

And do not participate in the unfruitful deeds of darkness, but instead even expose them; for it is disgraceful even to speak of the things which are done by them in secret.

Just refusing to participate in the deeds of darkness can be hard enough for Christians, but going to the next level and even exposing them is a code of honor which very few have been able to live by.

It is hard to know where the line is drawn between a critical person with a religious spirit, who is trying to find out what everyone else is doing wrong, and one standing for the truth and righteousness which should be the constitution of every Christian. This is an important issue which will become even more so as the ultimate conflict between light and darkness unfolds.

So how do we know where the line is? First, the answer is not a formula, but rather a Person we are seeking to follow—the Holy Spirit. When we come to know and love the Holy Spirit, we will come to know and love true holiness because that is His basic nature. When we begin to perceive *true holiness,* not the counterfeit rooted in a religious spirit, holiness will become the desire of our hearts. True holiness, when demonstrated with the grace and dignity inherent in the truth, will attract others, not repel them.

In Psalm 29:2 we are told to "**...worship the LORD in the beauty of holiness**" (KJV). There is a beauty, dignity, and nobility to true holiness which makes it one of the most compelling graces on earth. As we begin to walk in true holiness, others will be drawn by its beauty and nobility, being convicted that this is the way they too were created to live.

In contrast to the beauty of holiness, there is rigidity, harshness, and pride attached to the counterfeit of holiness, the "religious spirit," which is ugly and repelling. This is why Jesus, the most holy person to ever walk the earth, attracted some of the worst sinners, and only repelled those who were living by the counterfeit: the religious spirit, unrighteous political ambitions, or economic greed. Those who are caught in the grip of these unholy spiritual yokes will resist truth, and we should not be surprised when they do. In fact, we should take their opposition as encouragement.

When Jesus walked the earth He drew sinners to Himself, and yet He did convict them of their sin. It is interesting that He usually did this by first forgiving them, and often curing them of the afflictions which were the result of their sin. To be really effective in convicting sinners of sin, we need such mercy, grace, and compassion—a hallmark of the holiness which we know is the result of the grace of God being given to us, and not our own works. Because we have been forgiven and changed, we can have compassion on others, and will be prone to seek their healing and restoration rather than their condemnation. God's mercy and grace can be far more convicting than threats of judgment. That is why we are told in Romans 2:3-4:

> **And do you suppose this, O man, when you pass judgment upon those who practice such things and do the same yourself, that you will escape the judgment of God?**

Or do you think lightly of the riches of His kindness and forbearance and patience, not knowing that the kindness of God leads you to repentance?

True repentance almost always begins with the realization of God's love and mercy. However, this is the result of coming to grips with the judgment that we deserve, and the price which Jesus paid for our salvation. We cannot truly understand His kindness until we come to grips with how evil we are and how much He still loves us. So the standard which brings about true repentance is an uncompromising standard of His righteousness, but it is hoisted by the cross—the most profound and compelling demonstration of the love and mercy of God, that He laid down His own life for our salvation.

The next verses in our study Ephesians 5:13-14, take this to another level:

But all things become visible when they are exposed by the light, for everything that becomes visible is light.

For this reason it says, "Awake, sleeper, and arise from the dead, and Christ will shine on you."

When the light of the impending day of the Lord dawns, it is going to make all things visible. One of the key effects that we can expect, and are experiencing in these last days, is the exposure of things that are hidden. This is because of the increasing light which is now shining on the earth from the impending dawn of the day of the Lord. Because of this, we can expect a continuing and increasing exposure of political, business, and religious scandals. However, as the second verse declares, this should not discourage us, but rather be a call to wake up because the day is certainly at hand.

It is also true that it gets the darkest just before the dawn, and the coldest hour of the day is usually the one in which the sun rises. This is also the time when the love of many will grow cold. But the one thousand year day in which the Lord will rule over this earth is coming as surely as the sun rises each morning.

What do you see—darkness or light? What do you feel—coldness or the promise of warmth?

As one friend of mine said, "For seventy years the communists said, 'There is no God.' Then the Lord said, 'There is no communism!'" and in a single year the world changed more dramatically than it had in almost any previous century. That was from just the smallest ray of light from the impending dawn. What will the full dawn be like? We can be sure that every evil, spiritual stronghold which exalts itself against the knowledge of God will crumble, regardless of how bold and desperate it may become for a while.

One thing we can also count on during this time is the devil being more stirred up than ever, as we are told in Revelation 12:12, **"For this reason, rejoice, O heavens and you who dwell in them. Woe to the earth and the sea, because the devil has come down to you, having great wrath, knowing that he has only a short time."** Just as some of history's most cruel despots have done their cruelest deeds in their final hours, we can expect the devil to do the same.

Even so, for those who are awake, they will not be surprised by these things, but will work even more zealously so that the Lord will find faith on the earth when He comes. We are living in the times of the greatest conflict between light and darkness, but the light will surely prevail! So let us stay awake at our post, not letting our guard down, but standing for truth, for righteousness, and for the gospel, being encouraged that the time of its ultimate victory is certainly near.

As the next verses in our study, Ephesians 5:15-17, state:

Therefore be careful how you walk, not as unwise men, but as wise,

making the most of your time, because the days are evil.

So then do not be foolish, but understand what the will of the Lord is.

As someone once said, "Whenever you see a 'therefore' in Scripture, go back and see what it is *there for.*" This verse is a continuation of the ones we addressed about how everything will be made visible by the light. We must arise so that the light of Christ can shine on us. Once we arise, or awake for the day, we must be careful how we walk. Two ways we do this are by not wasting our time and by understanding what the will of the Lord is.

It is tragic that most teachings on the end times revolve more around the anti-Christ than Christ. Most books I have read on the book of Revelation give far more emphasis on the anti-Christ than Christ. This is done even though, as stated in the very first verse, this revelation was given to John as **"The Revelation of Jesus Christ..." (Revelation 1:1).** We will never have a right eschatology by interpreting everything according to what we think the anti-Christ is going to do. All true understanding will come from how "the light of Christ" shines on us.

Even so, it is crucial that we are careful how we walk, and as our text for this chapter declares, wise men will walk making the most of their time. Time is one of the most valuable gifts we have been given, and we do not know how much of it we have. Even so, just being perpetually occupied is not the way we wisely use our time. We can be very busy, but accomplishing nothing worthwhile if we do not understand what the will of the Lord is. This should be the primary question that our lives revolve around: What is the will of the Lord?

To review one of the most basic issues about how to know the will of the Lord, we are told in Romans 12:2, **"And do not be conformed to this world, but be transformed by the renewing of your mind, that you may prove what the will of God is..."** We cannot understand what the will of God is for us as long as we are thinking the way the world thinks. Therefore, having our minds renewed so we think as the Lord thinks, seeing with His eyes, hearing with His ears, and understanding with His heart, is fundamental to the true Christian walk.

So, what is having the greatest effect on our thinking? Is it the news media? Is it what our secular teachers taught us? Or is it the ways of the Lord as revealed in the Scripture? I have been shocked over and over by how many supposedly solid Christians, even Christian leaders will hold to human philosophies that are in blatant conflict with the Scriptures, and will remain stubbornly resolute in their humanistic convictions even when shown the Scriptures refuting their positions. This is one of the things we can be sure about—the light of Christ is going to be revealing more and more of how weak the foundations of many Christians and churches are because they have not really had their minds renewed. As the Lord warned in Matthew 6:23b, **"If therefore the light that is in you is darkness, how great is the darkness!"**

It is unquestionably the forming of our minds according the humanistic and worldly philosophies rather than sound biblical truth which is the number one reason why so many Christians remain in such confusion about the will of God in their life. If our minds have been transformed, we will not only know what the will of the Lord is, we will be able to prove it! (see Romans 12:2). There are none on earth who should be living with more boldness, peace, and success than Christians. However, this requires thinking very differently than others do. Can that be said of us?

CHAPTER SIX

Being Filled
with the Spirit

In this chapter we will continue our study with Ephesians 5:18:

> **And do not get drunk with wine, for that is dissipation, but be filled with the Spirit.**

If Paul were writing this today he would almost certainly add to the admonition to not be drunk with wine, "neither be stoned on drugs." Neither of these are acceptable behavior for a son and daughter of the King. They are not only counterfeits of being filled with the Spirit, but are wide open doors for evil spirits to enter into our lives to deceive and mislead us.

The primary effects of intoxication are the loss of judgment and a flawed understanding (see Isaiah 28:7, Hosea 4:11). As we read in Proverbs 23:29-33, those who **"linger long over wine"** will have **"woe, sorrow, contentions, complaining,"** and **"wounds without cause."** And he added that it **"... goes down smoothly,"** but **"bites like a serpent, and stings like a viper. Your eyes will see strange things, and your mind will utter perverse things."** The other results of the abuse of alcohol that are stated by Scripture are:

1) poverty (see Proverbs 23:21),

2) a mal-administration of justice (see Proverbs 31:5, Isaiah 5:22-23),

3) anger, contention, and brawling (see Proverbs 20:1; 23:29),

4) a life of dissipation (see Ephesians 5:18),

5) an alliance with gambling, licentiousness, and indecency (see Joel 3:3, Genesis 9:21) and,

6) deadening the spiritual sensibilities, producing a callous indifference to God, and destroying all serious thought (see Isaiah 5:11-12).

So why would any believer who is committed to a fruitful, productive, and godly life, ever touch wine? The first argument that is usually made is that the Lord Jesus Himself drank wine, and even promises that we will drink it in the kingdom (see Matthew 26:29, Isaiah 25:6). If the effects of wine are so evil, as we saw in all of the previous Scriptures, why would the Lord Himself drink it, or even have it in the kingdom?

Some have tried to reconcile this seeming conflict by saying that Jesus did not really drink wine, but grape juice. Any person who is committed to truth and sound, biblical doctrine will have to acknowledge this is not the case, and such reasoning has cost those who hold to it their credibility with anyone who can think or search the Scriptures for themselves. Regardless of how much we do not understand something, or do not agree with it, we must never bend either the Scriptures or sound reasoning to establish a true doctrine. Why would His enemies have called Jesus a "drunkard or a winebibber" (see Matthew 11:19) if He was only drinking grape juice? The truth is that He did drink real wine. His first miracle was to make some obviously very good wine, and real wine is going to be served in the kingdom.

The truth is that nowhere do the Scriptures condemn the drinking of wine, but it is the excessive drinking, being intoxicated by it, which is condemned. There are Scriptures that commend the production of wine, and drinking it in certain circumstances (see Proverbs 3:10; I Timothy 5:23).

Over the last few years a number of interesting studies have been published on alcoholism and wine drinking. One study found that the people group having the highest rate of alcoholism were members of denominations which forbid drinking any form of alcohol. The group which had the lowest percentage of alcoholism were the Jewish people who have no such prohibitions. My point in bringing this up is that doctrines and the traditions of men which go beyond clear biblical guidelines will never result in righteousness, but will in fact excite sin as Paul warned about this in his Epistles to the Romans and Corinthians. Those who hold to such teachings, which go beyond a clear biblical mandate, do also usually become modern Pharisees, who look good on the outside but are full of death on the inside.

Another major study found that the drinking of very modest amounts of wine at least four times a week can substantially reduce one's cholesterol level. I know of one well-known man of God whose doctor prescribed a glass of red wine for him each day and the result was it reduced his cholesterol in just a few weeks by 70 points. I have heard many other such personal reports. This is why the French, who tend to eat some of the richest foods, have a remarkably low amount of heart disease compared to any other nation. Every study done on this points to the reason being that they drink wine with their meals. In contrast to this, the so-called "Bible belt" has been called "the stroke belt" because the drinking of wine has been so condemned.

Am I trying to justify the drinking of wine? Yes, because it is clear in the Scriptures that the Lord drinks wine. Even so, I can also understand how anyone who has seen the destruction of people and their families by alcohol would tend to be so against it, even to the point of bending the Scriptures and sound reasoning a bit. Yet, this still does not make trying to justify our position in this way right or true.

It is also both wise and biblical, that anyone who has been an alcoholic, or is to any degree lacking self-control in the matter, should stay far away from wine or any other form of alcohol. Even if they have high cholesterol, there are other ways to reduce it which would be much better for them. It is also not right for a believer, who has the liberty to drink wine in moderation to exercise that liberty around those who have problems with alcohol, as the Scriptures also make clear (see Romans 14:21).

Again, our verse for this chapter does not tell us not to drink wine, but rather not to be drunk with it. The reason is so we can be filled with the Spirit. Anyone who has experienced being filled with the Spirit would never want to do anything that would dull their sensitivity to Him. This is not just about feeling good, but it is about walking in the light, in the truth. Any form of intoxication subjects us to delusion, deception, and other evil influences.

Though the Scriptures make it very clear that Jesus did drink real wine, we can also be sure He at no time ever drank it to be intoxicated, or to be stimulated mentally or physically. As the Lord said in Matthew 11:18-19:

> **"For John came neither eating nor drinking, and they say, 'He has a demon!'**
>
> **The Son of Man came eating and drinking, and they say, 'Behold, a gluttonous man and a drunkard, a friend of tax-gatherers and sinners!' Yet wisdom is vindicated by her deeds."**

Someone will condemn you for taking either side of this argument. As for me, there are things which are clearly forbidden in Scripture that I have resolved to be resolute in standing against, but for all other things I have resolved to guard the liberty which has been given to us under the New Covenant. It is also true that moderation can be a greater witness than abstinence. Liberty under the grace of self-control is a far better testimony than legalism. Being filled with the Spirit is even greater.

CHAPTER SEVEN

Music and the Spiritual Mind

N ow we proceed to a very interesting verse, Ephesians 5:19:

speaking to one another in psalms and hymns and spiritual songs, singing and making melody with your heart to the Lord;

Music has been called the only universal language. This is because it can go beyond the mind to touch the heart, the emotions, and therefore communicate in something other than language. This is why it is one of the most powerful media on earth, and why the devil has made it one of his most powerful weapons. However, we must realize that the Lord has also used it as one of His most powerful weapons. We can also be sure that music belongs to the Lord, not the devil, and one of the important mandates of our time is to retake music for the kingdom.

Another one of the devil's greatest victories over Christians has been the promotion of doctrines which cause us to think that God does not want to move us through our emotions, but only through our will. It is true that He wants us to have a will which is strong and resolute to walk in righteousness and do His will, but there is much more to the Christian life than just obedience— there is worship, and worship is profoundly emotional.

How would you like it if your spouse came to you and said, "Darling, I don't feel anything for you, but I love you out of obedience to the Lord?" How does the Lord feel when we sing songs to Him with no emotion? To do so must be the ultimate demonstration of a soul gripped by the Laodicean lukewarmness.

Obedience does come from the will, but worship comes from the heart, the emotions. That is why the Lord said in John 4:24, **"God is spirit, and those who worship Him must worship in spirit and truth."** If our worship is devoid of emotion, then it is less than a waste of time—it is hypocrisy.

So how do we speak to one another in psalms, hymns, and spiritual songs? Does this mean when we meet each other on the street we should sing our conversations to each other? I don't think that is what the apostle meant. This is a directive to put messages into song. In this way, the message can touch the heart as well as the mind and therefore go much deeper. This is why the great hymns are those which proclaim the great truths of the faith. Some have a deep and powerful theology, and others have great teachings that edify those who sing them. The great Christian songs are the ones that have depth of content in their words as well.

We must also recognize that this verse is an exhortation not to just sing to the Lord, but to His people as well. One of the ways we worship or serve the Lord, is by serving His family, the church.

When the Lord first started giving our worship leaders at MorningStar a new direction in our music, we did not know what to call it. Most of our songs were exhortations to the church to stand for truth and righteousness, or to resist the evil strongholds which were capturing so many of the Lord's people. Some, who feel all worship should stir an adoration for the Lord which promotes intimacy with Him, did not like our music, which we could understand. However, we had spent many years laying that foundation. We believe the Lord is leading us in the way that we are going.

Just as King David was one of the greatest worshipers in Scripture, as well as one of the greatest warriors, we were told it was now time for war. We finally started calling our music war-ship instead of worship. Most of the songs were not the kind which drew you into deep intimacy with the Lord, but rather instilled a resolve to stand for truth and righteousness, and against the great evils of our times. Since that time we have gone through different stages in our music, but there remains militancy in both the beat and words. Even the songs which are intended to promote intimacy with the Lord tend to have aggressiveness to them. These are born out of a fellowship of people who are aggressively pursuing the Lord and His kingdom. There are other churches and ministries that are speaking other things through their psalms and hymns, which is their message, and this too is right for them because it reflects who they are.

When I visit a church or ministry to speak, I often do not know what my message to them will be until I hear their worship service. I can often tell by the songs they sing what the Lord is doing in them at that time. This is not always the case, but it usually will be if there is harmony between the worship leader and what is going on in the church body. In this way I try to discern what the Lord is doing in the church so I will only plant seeds I know will get watered, or water seeds that have already been planted. My goal is never to just have a good message, but a relevant one which bears fruit.

In this same way we can tell much about where the world is headed by the music that is popular. By this we can also at times discern the schemes of the devil. We can also discern how the Lord sometimes speaks to the world through secular music, using it to reach those who do not know Him.

The bottom line is that songs are spiritual, and a powerful medium of communication. The church must learn to use this media skillfully for it is a very powerful weapon, as well as a wonderful and powerful vehicle to communicate love.

CHAPTER EIGHT

Dwelling in His Presence

In this chapter we will look at the next verse in this great epistle, Ephesians 5:20:

always giving thanks for all things in the name of our Lord Jesus Christ to God, even the Father;

The first three words of this verse are crucial for the victorious Christian's life–**"always giving thanks."** Does he really mean **"always?"** Why should we thank God for problems or for the attacks of the devil?

There are several good reasons for this which we looked at previously in Psalm 100:4. **"Enter His gates with thanksgiving, and His courts with praise."** The best way to dwell in the presence of the Lord is to be a thankful person. As we thank Him we enter His gates. As we go further and begin to praise Him we go deeper into His courts.

Likewise, one of the quickest ways to be disqualified from living in the promises of the Lord is to be a complainer, which is one of the reasons the first generation that left Egypt was not able to enter the Promised Land (see I Corinthians 10:10). Complaining is the language of doubt and unbelief. Thanksgiving is the language of faith. Remember our words have power— prophetic power. Someone once said, "You should always make your words sweet because you never know when you will have to eat them!"

To be a successful leader in almost any field, one of the first things you have to do is either remove the complaining or the complainers from among those you are leading. Business leaders are taught how to recognize and either isolate or remove problem-oriented people, and replace them with solution-oriented people. Successful coaches of sports teams will all agree that if the most talented person on their team is a complainer, they will trade him any time for a much less-talented person who has a good attitude. If you don't get rid of the complainers, you will end up with the same problem that Israel faced at Kadesh-Barnea, where the ten fearful, whining, complaining spies cost an entire generation their inheritance in the Lord. The two good spies saw all of the same problems the ten evil spies saw, but they had a very different attitude about them.

Christians are given one of the greatest promises ever in Romans 8:28, **"And we know that God causes all things to work together for good to those who love God, to those who are called according to His purpose."** Therefore, how could we ever complain about anything He allows if we believe this? It is only when we have been deceived into believing the lie, that everything is going bad for us, that we would ever complain.

Psalm 100:5 gives us a very good reason to always be thankful. **"For the LORD is good; His lovingkindness is everlasting, and His faithfulness to all generations."** God is almighty. He could do anything or be any way He wanted. Yet, just think of how wonderful it is that He did not just destroy the earth and mankind after the Fall, but gave His own Son for our salvation! For Jesus to have left the glory and presence of the Father in heaven to come to earth and live among us, to suffer the cross, and then allow us to start again by being born again, giving us His Holy Spirit, and then to put up with all we do after we have been born again and received His Spirit, is incredible! Even then, He causes everything to work together for our good. What an awesome, wonderful God we have! How can we not be thankful? Eternity will not be long enough to thank Him.

The next verse in our study, Ephesians 5:21, states: **"and be subject to one another in the fear of Christ."** This may seem a bit disconnected from the first verse we studied in this chapter, but it really is not when we think of how we must thank the Lord for **"all things."**

The teachings of the Lord such as John 5:44, and Paul in Ephesians 1:10, make it clear that one of the most corruptive and destructive forces in the lives of those who seek to serve the Lord is the fear of man. However, this chapter's verse commands us to **"be subject to one another."** How can we do this and not be seduced by the fear of man?

This verse tells us how. We submit ourselves to one another **"in the fear of Christ,"** not the fear of man. Isn't this a bit confusing? How can we tell the difference? It is easy. If we are living in the fear of man, we will get our encouragement or discouragement by how people feel about us. If we are living in the fear of God, our overwhelming concern will be to please Him in all that we do, and we will be neither very discouraged or encouraged by what people think of us.

Even so, this verse declares that we should be subject to one another. There are some who seek to live free of the fear of man, but do it more out of a spirit of rebellion and arrogance than the fear of the Lord, true faith, or being humble, that God gives His grace to. This is where many people who are seeking to serve the Lord stumble. These will also usually end up doing more damage to the church and to the kingdom than good, sowing division and rebellion instead of the pure and holy fear of God.

Those who fall into this trap usually do so because they fail to recognize that the Lord does almost everything on the earth through His body. The leadership He gives to His body is His leadership in His body. If we are going to be subject to the Lord, we must learn to recognize and submit to His delegated authority, and to do so as unto Him. This is most difficult because none of His delegated authorities are Him, or are nearly as good, true, perfect, or powerful as He is. As James said, **"We all stumble in many ways..." (James 3:2).** The leaders that the Lord has delegated over His work on the earth do stumble in many ways. It therefore requires an even greater humility to be subject to them, which is an opportunity for the Lord to give us an even greater grace.

Think about the apostles the Lord left in charge of His church after His ascension. They had just denied Him and scattered when He needed His friends the most. The people who were gathered to the Lord and who were to be built upon the apostles' teaching were all very aware of this in their leaders. Yet they trusted them, and submitted to them. Why? Because they were not just putting their trust in these men, but in the Holy Spirit who was in them. They were the ones the Lord had given to them as leaders, so they must be the right ones—not perfect, just right for the job. The apostles, also being humbled by their previous failures, were then even more able to be the recipients of God's grace and anointing.

Which one of us, who is so demanding of perfection in those we will follow, are therefore perfect enough to lead? That very attitude is the pride which comes before the fall. It is therefore the fear of the Lord which enables us to be subject to one another rightly. If we are wise we will learn to cover our brothers' and sisters' flaws, knowing that if we will sow grace we will reap the same.

If you really want to know how humble you are, think about how you reacted to the last person who offered you advice, or even correction, whom you perceived to be less spiritual than you are. One of the great attributes of King David was that as he was fleeing from his rebellious son, Absalom, he would not even stop a mad man from throwing stones at him until he had first determined that the Lord had not sent this deranged man as a messenger. This would be remarkable for anyone, much less a king. It is true that after he had determined that this was not from the Lord, he had the man taken care of, which had to be done for the sake of protecting the kingdom from madness and rebellion.

I have heard many people say they love the Lord, but they just do not like the church. According to Scripture that is not possible, as we read in 1 John 4:20, **"... the one who does not love his brother whom he has seen, cannot love God whom he has not seen."** This same principle is true with authority. We cannot be subject to God who we cannot see, if we are not subject to His people, who we can see.

CHAPTER NINE

The High Calling to Be a Wife

In this chapter we will study one of the more interesting texts in this Epistle, especially for modern times, Ephesians 5:22-24:

> **Wives, be subject to your own husbands, as to the Lord.**

> **For the husband is the head of the wife, as Christ also is the head of the church, He Himself being the Savior of the body.**

> **But as the church is subject to Christ, so also the wives ought to be to their husbands in everything.**

Could the Lord actually mean for wives to be subject to their husbands **"as to the Lord?"** Could He really mean **"in everything?"** Certainly in modern times it is controversial to teach that wives should be subject to their husbands at all. I am asked quite frequently if I think this is really what the Lord meant, or if they should actually try to obey it. My answer is always the same—I do not think women should have to be subject to their husbands...unless they want their marriage to last, and they want the blessing of God on it.

That may sound like an extreme statement, but it is true. Let's face it, the modern Western approach to marriage which negates the clear mandate that God stated in the verses above is causing the destruction of the very institution of marriage. This is happening to such a degree that there are many who now believe the institution of marriage will not survive the twenty-first century. The pressures on marriages are growing. Those which are not built upon the rock of both hearing and obeying the Word of God will not survive the storm.

This may seem like a contradiction at this point, but the Lord has not limited women in any way. They can walk in just as much anointing or authority as any man. God is absolutely for women's liberation. He is for it much more than the modern women's liberation movement. However, to those who have not yet had their minds renewed, God's way to liberation will appear at first to be the way to bondage, and the devil's path to bondage will appear as the path to liberation.

To those whose minds have been shaped more by the world than by the Spirit, our verses for this chapter are considered one of the most sexist texts in the Bible. However, to the renewed mind that is spiritual, it is one of the more liberating texts in the Bible for women. If you cannot see this, then your mind has not yet been renewed as it should be. In any thing where we do not agree with the Word of God and His wisdom, we still have a darkened mind, which is more in agreement with the spirit of the world than with God.

One misconception implied in these verses is that all men have authority over all women. This is not the case. These verses are specifically addressing the home and family. God has ordained for the husband to be the head of the home, and without seeing this, and living by it, our home will never be what God intended it to be, or have the blessing on it He intended it to have. In any area of our lives where we are being disobedient, it opens us wide to the attacks of the devil, and you can count on him going after your marriage if he can.

I have no trouble with women as heads of ministries, churches, corporations, or heads of state. One of my favorite world leaders was Margaret Thatcher, the former Prime Minister of Great Britain. However, a woman who is the President should still submit to her husband as the head of her home. That may sound crazy, but it is wisdom, and it is doable. We do not have the space here to address this subject in the way that it deserves, but I do want to get a little basic and practical.

First, being the head of the home does not mean you do not or should not listen to the counsel of your wife, and children too, for that matter. Neither does it mean that you should not delegate authority, even to keep the checkbook. I do know many women who are not gifted in financial matters and should not keep the family checkbook, but I know just as many men in the same category. I know pastors, heads of ministries, and corporate leaders whose wives are more gifted in financial matters than they are. These should let their wives keep the checkbook at home, and get a good Chief Financial Officer for their ministry or business. They can still make the general, financial policy or have ultimate authority over major decisions. Even so, we are called to **"be subject to one another"** in Christ, which means that we should acknowledge and submit to each other's gifts and anointings. We can do this and still be the "head."

Also, there is something very sexually seductive to most men about a submissive woman. If a man comes home at night to a wife who is domineering, challenging, or disrespectful, he will be wide open to the attraction of a submissive secretary. This is not to justify infidelity under any circumstances, but this is a major scheme of the enemy that he has used effectively countless times. He will use it on your marriage if he possibly can.

A wife who tries to make her husband feel like a king in his home will usually find him treating her like a queen, and he will be far less likely to be attracted to others. Men who feel belittled or not respected by their wives will likely lose their attraction to her, and start being attracted to those who show them respect. It is a fact.

One reason so many wives have determined to resist the mandate of our verses for this chapter, or ignore it, is because the images these verses bring to their minds are often of the abuses of domineering husbands. There are those who abuse every truth, take them to extremes, or use them for their own selfish reasons. Nevertheless, this does not negate the truth or our responsibility to obey it.

Another basic misunderstanding of those whose minds are not yet renewed is how the Lord's authority is given for the purpose of being a servant instead of just lording it over others. Paul is establishing here that the husband is to be the servant of the wife, but the application of this is different than in the world, as spiritual realities usually are.

We can be sure of one thing—there is no greater liberty which we can ever know than doing things God's way. He created us, and He knows better than we ever could what is best for us. Without this basic faith in God, we do not really have faith.

God not only made men and women different physically, but they are called to have different roles in the home. These differences do not conflict with each other, but complete each other. One is strong where the other has need, and vice versa. This is so they could be the team that they are called to be.

One of the most concerted attacks of the devil in our times is to blur the distinctions between men and women so that neither can be who God created them to be. Yet, the Lord Jesus, and the apostles, began the first true women's liberation movement on the earth. They exalted the role of women far beyond anything previously considered, and probably even more than has been perceived in our times.

The Scripture is clear that "**...where the Spirit of the Lord is, there is liberty" (II Corinthians 3:17).** This is not just intended for some, but for all of creation. We will never know greater freedom than being who God created us to be. However, liberty the way the world perceives it and true liberty can be very different.

A train may want to be free of its tracks to go wandering across the countryside, but it would quickly bog down and not be able to go anywhere. The tracks that seem to restrain and bind it are what really make the train free to be what it was created to be. We are much the same. There is no greater freedom than to know the boundaries which God has set for us so that we can freely move within them with great confidence.

We must also recognize that spiritual authority is much greater than authority which is exercised in regard to matters of this life. In the Old Testament there was a separation of the secular authority of the king from the spiritual authority of the priesthood, and they still need to be separated in many ways. A woman who can be freed of some of the secular authority, can be devoted more to the spiritual authority which can accomplish much more.

One of the devastating doctrines which emerged in some movements during the 1970s was that the man was "the priest" of his home. All believers are called to be priests, which includes both men and women. In fact, women in general tend to be better intercessors and priests in the home than men. When this doctrine circulated, it was devastating to the effective ministry of the priesthood not only in the home, but in the church as well. It would have been better for a doctrine to have been circulated saying the woman is the priest of the home and the man is the head, but together they form the ministry of the home as God desires it.

There are few greater demonstrations of the grace of God, faith in God, and the majesty of the human being created in the image of God, than a godly, feminine, submissive woman. "Submission" is one of those words that the devil has likewise worked over-time to distort because it is such a powerful demonstration of both grace and true authority in our lives. There have certainly been, and continues to be, many extremes in the application of this word, and because of this many have been swinging to the opposite extreme of lawlessness. Again, we must remember that there is a ditch on either side of the path of life.

Submission is in many ways one of the greatest demonstrations of faith. A godly woman who is submitted to a godly husband is one of the great examples of the relationship the church is called to have with the Lord. A godly woman who is submitted to an ungodly husband can be an even greater demonstration of faith, and can by this be one of the most powerful means of winning not only her husband, but others as well. This is not to imply that a godly woman should submit to things which are ungodly, unlawful, or abusive. But even when resisting, if it is done with respect for her husband, and not in a rebellious spirit, it will be a powerful means of conviction.

If the man is not the head of the home, carrying the authority and final word on matters relating to the family, that family is out of order. However, if the man is not loving his wife like Christ loved the church, then the home is still out of order, which we will cover in more detail in the next chapter.

Where does this leave families when the father is no longer present? The Lord Jesus Himself is the answer to every human problem, and His grace is sufficient for any situation. As Psalm 68:5 declares, **"A father of the fatherless and a judge for the widows, is God in His holy habitation."** The way the Lord wants to provide for such needs is through **"His holy habitation,"** which is the church.

Again, there is much more to this subject than we can cover in a short chapter. The way I have addressed this here may have left you with more questions than answers. That was at least part of my intent. The answers to this issue are right, true, and perfect, when God's counsel is found. The world is throwing a host of its answers and philosophies at the subject too, and the result of this unrelenting attack upon family relationships has been the destruction of a multitude of families. If we are going to be a part of preparing for the coming of the kingdom instead of the devil's strategy to destroy, whether we are the husband or the wife, we must remember the exhortation of Mark 8:34-35:

"If anyone wishes to come after Me, let him deny himself, and take up his cross, and follow Me.

"For whoever wishes to save his life shall lose it; but whoever loses his life for My sake and the gospel's shall save it.

In this chapter we have been dealing with the text concerning the wife. In the next chapter we will deal with the husband. The marriage relationship will almost certainly be either heaven or hell. You can be sure of one thing—the Lord is not just trying to change you—He is trying to kill you! One of the primary ways He has chosen to accomplish this is marriage. Your marriage can be heaven on earth if you will just die, renouncing your self-life to serve your spouse. It will be hell if you seek to save your self-life in your marriage, and it will not likely survive long under the modern pressures and stresses it must endure.

CHAPTER TEN

The High Calling to Be a Husband

In this chapter we continue our study with Ephesians 5:25-29:

> **Husbands, love your wives, just as Christ also loved the church and gave Himself up for her;**
>
> **that He might sanctify her, having cleansed her by the washing of water with the word,**
>
> **that He might present to Himself the church in all her glory, having no spot or wrinkle or any such thing; but that she should be holy and blameless.**
>
> **So husbands ought also to love their own wives as their own bodies. He who loves his own wife loves himself;**
>
> **for no one ever hated his own flesh, but nourishes and cherishes it, just as Christ also does the church,**

Along with the verses we examined in the last chapter, this concludes the Bible's most important marriage counseling. It is also interesting that the only marriage counselor in the Bible was not even married! Was this because he could give a more objective view? In the view of some skeptics it is because it is much easier to preach things you don't have to personally try to live up to! He certainly did lay out some very high standards in marriage for both husbands and wives. However, one thing we can be sure of—this is the Word of God. For the true believer, compromising them, or making excuses for them, is not an option.

The verses from the last chapter and this chapter together basically say that the woman should respect and obey her husband as the church does the Lord, and that the husband should love and serve his wife as Christ does the church. The fulfillment of this will make the Christian marriage one of the great witnesses of the relationship that the Lord has with His people.

Certainly, to have a godly marriage that comes anywhere close to these standards is a remarkable thing today, even among Christians. In fact, recent studies have revealed that evangelical Christians are now divorcing at a rate faster than non-believers. Why is this happening?

The main reason is probably because the devil's main assault on humanity at this time is directed at destroying the family. Man is a social creature. After the Lord had created man He said, **"It is not good for the man to be alone" (Genesis 2:18).** This is very interesting because man had God for fellowship at this time. Our relationship to God is even more basic than our human needs, but God created us to also need each other. The family is the most basic social structure. To the degree that the devil can weaken or destroy this relationship, will be the degree to which he can destabilize, and then destroy mankind. This is his intent.

Destroying mankind, or getting us to destroy each other is the devil's basic ambition. Restoring mankind to the purpose for which we were created is God's basic design. The family is one of the central and most important battlegrounds where this strategic conflict is waged for the destiny of mankind.

This ploy of the devil to destroy the family will not work because ultimately there will be faithful ones who during the greatest onslaught will rise to the greatest obedience. Right now the intensity of the onslaught is causing a great separation to take place between the truly faithful, and those who are lukewarm. Just as the Lord said that the lukewarm would be spewed out of His mouth, they are even right now being spewed out of His kingdom. As the onslaught of lawlessness increases, it will be a miracle if anyone can stand. That is the point—everyone who is standing for truth and righteousness will be miracles, and the whole world, and ultimately even the principalities and powers in the heavenly places, will acknowledge them as such.

During this increasing darkness those who do stand, whose marriages survive, will not only be survivors but glorious testimonies of what God desired the marriage relationship to be. The ones who are just barely "hanging on" are going to have an increasingly difficult time. Soon everyone who is not gaining ground will be losing it. The ones who prevail are going to be the ones who are built on the Word of God. As the Lord taught, it will only be those who built their houses on hearing and obeying the Word of God who will stand the coming storm.

If the Word of God, and the standards of what God has called the marriage relationship to be offend you now, you or your marriage will not make it through what is coming. We must make a choice as to whether we are going to live by the human philosophies and standards of the day, or by God's.

As I have also often said, there is a ditch on either side of the path of life. It may at first seem like a contradiction to what I have been saying, but a main reason for the meltdown of Christian marriages today is the idealistic interpretation of the Word of God in relation to Christian marriage. This idealism has caused many to promote standards for both wives and husbands that no one can live up to. This causes frustration and a continual feeling of defeat which only weakens marriages.

I rarely talk to a husband or wife who has been reading a Christian book about marriage who is not frustrated with their spouse because they are not living up to the ideals presented in the book. Of course, it is obvious that if their spouse would also read the book, they would be just as frustrated with them for not measuring up to their part either. This is often the fault line (pun intended) that begins the break up of the marriage. What is the answer?

First, I think we need to lower our expectations in marriage. I am not saying this for shock effect; I am saying it because I believe it is true. Last Mother's Day we asked several of the mothers in our local congregation to share what they would like to have for Mother's Day. We were expecting them to share some things that their children could do for them. It was Mother's Day and not "Wife's Day," but almost all of their requests were directed at the husbands. I do not think a single husband could have lived up to those requests without quitting his job, giving up all his time for the Lord, his children, recreation, and everything to love and serve his wife. Even so, the women who shared these things were honestly wanting what they had requested.

Now on Father's Day we got even. There was little hope for any wife who had children, a home, relationship to the Lord, much less a job, or any outside relationships, to live up to what the husbands wanted their wives to be like. I hope this was a revelation to all in our congregation; we need to start by giving grace to each other, and determine that we are not going to have unrealistic expectations of one another.

However, I am not by this trying to compromise the standards the Scriptures teach for the marriage. I only think we need to understand it may take our entire marriage to attain them. By this I mean if the Lord knows we are going to live to be married for fifty years, it may take that long for us to get there. Sound crazy? Not as crazy as trying to get there immediately.

Doesn't my proposal mean that we will only be witnesses of what marriage is supposed to be like for maybe one year? Maybe. And that may be enough. However, I think the truth may be somewhere between these two extremes.

I am not saying it will take decades to have a biblical marriage. I think everyone who seeks to obey the Lord and His mandate can have a glorious relationship from the beginning, and at each stage along the way. Even so, we need to understand that as we are born again we are just starting to grow up into all we are to be in Christ. When we are first married we are just starting to learn how to be husbands and wives. Even though the Lord has done just about every kind of miracle imaginable, I do not see anywhere in Scripture where He makes anyone mature instantly! Just as being a mature Christian takes maturing, so does having a mature marriage.

Coach Bill McCartney, the founder of Promise Keepers, shared something in our last Pastors and Leader's Conference which was eye opening to many. He said that just recently his wife had said that he had finally become the husband she had always dreamed of having. They are now in their sixties. It took them decades to get there. He was trying the whole time, and was on the road to getting there, but every journey requires time.

It was interesting to me that Coach never mentioned whether his wife had just begun to live up to his expectations of a wife, because it was obvious he was much more intent on whether he was living up to his part than thinking about whether she was living up to her part. I do think this is the way it should be for husbands. The Scriptures seem clear that the greatest responsibility for making the marriage into what it should be does lie with the man.

My simple proposal for complying with the biblical mandate of Ephesians 5 for marriage is to give yourself time. Know that in your first year of marriage you are going to have an immature marriage, and this is okay! It is okay for a one-year old to be one. Enjoy growing up, and don't try to rush it too much.

Many marriages have stayed at the same level or even slid backwards for years. Maybe you have been married twenty years now and have not really made much progress for the last fifteen. This is often the case when children come. However, you have probably made more progress than you think, though you may feel more frustrated in your marriage now. Even if you become convicted and know you have to do something, I encourage you not to try to make up the ground too fast. That can be counter-productive.

For example, if you have been convicted that you have not been having devotions with your family as you should have been, instead of trying to have daily devotions with your wife and children, start with weekly devotions. Also, keep them short. I would recommend something like fifteen minutes rather than an hour. If you are faithful, they will probably start to get so good that you will want to go longer, and then you will want to do it more often. It is much better to have shorter and fewer times with real life in them than longer and more frequent ones which are so boring and lifeless that they are viewed more as a punishment than an opportunity.

I realize I have very superficially touched on the verses for the last two chapters. Indeed, many books have been written on these verses, and they are worthy of many books. However, we obviously cannot do that here, so the main thing I have tried to accomplish is the appeal to "get real." We need to acknowledge our failures, and try to remove the unrealistic expectations which are rooted more in idealism than revelation. Then we need to develop a workable, step-by-step approach to a mature Christian marriage which can be achieved. We also need to determine that we will obey the Word of God and not try to rationalize it or ignore it. That is the only way we can build our house on the Rock.

CHAPTER ELEVEN

Members of His Body

As we have discussed, man was created to be a social creature. To be complete, we first need a relationship to God. Without this no human being can ever be all they were created to be. Next, we need relationships with other people. These can be of many different types and depths, but basically we were created to need both God and one another.

The ultimate fulfillment for both of these basic human needs in relationships is found in the body of Christ. A healthy church life is therefore essential for a healthy life. As it is intended to be, the church is the most brilliant, ingenious, powerful, social entity ever created. Of course, only God could have ever thought of such a thing which would fulfill the needs of man so perfectly.

Membership in social clubs does give some people a sense of identity and belonging. Membership in certain clubs can raise one's social standing. However, there is no club on earth which comes even close to being what the church is designed to be. Our verse for this week, Ephesians 5:30, emphasizes the most exalted, esteemed, and important group that anyone on earth could ever be joined to:

because we are members of His body.

The **"because"** in this verse refers to our studies of the previous two chapters—why men should love their wives as

Christ loves the church, and why women should respect their husbands even as they do the Lord. However, this **"because"** should also be the motivation for every endeavor of our lives.

For example, members of the United States Senate have to consider their position in almost everything they do. What they say about almost anything can carry weight because of their position. Their behavior can reflect on the whole nation for good or bad. How much more should our membership in the body of Christ govern our behavior and words?

In all of creation, Christ is the most exalted, except for the Father Himself. Even the most glorious and powerful angelic majesties bow in homage to Him. All authority in heaven and earth has been given to Him. There is not a President or king who has ever come close to the glory or majesty of our King. The most remarkable thing of all is that we are not just called to be His subjects, but to be actual members of His body—His very person! How much more should all we do be governed by this one thing?

Of course these terms are speaking metaphorically, just as we are also called His sheep, His bride, His city, His field, etc. Even so, these are metaphors which are intended to convey a profound truth. Just as we may think in our minds, but take action through the members of our bodies, Jesus does the same. When He moves on the earth He does it through His people.

The hand does not take its instructions from the leg, foot, or even the wrist which it is directly connected to, but gets its orders directly from the head. Every member of His body must likewise have his or her own direct communication with the Head. We may be joined to others, but we must all have a relationship to God which is direct as well.

It is true that the church has drifted far during what it was intended to be over the church age, but before the end of this age the body of Christ is going to arise to be all it was created to be. Just as we marvel at athletes who have remarkable coordination and ability, the whole world is going to marvel at the coordination and ability of the body of Christ. In fact, we can be sure no human body could ever match what the Lord is going to do through His body.

For this reason it is crucial for us to find our place in His body, and develop to the fullest our relationship with Him and His people. Basically this all comes down to relationships. If we are not growing in these relationships, then we are not growing toward our ultimate purpose.

Of course, as our text over the last couple of chapters has emphasized, our human relationships need to start with our marriages. But, this is not an "either/or" situation. Our marriages will not be healthy if we do not first have a relationship with the Lord and other members of His body. Those who overly focus on their marriage to the exclusion of others are only weakening their marriage.

We were designed to be the temple of the Lord, and just as His temple had three levels ranging from the highest level of intimacy in the Holy of Holies, to the Outer Court which let in just about everyone, we need to have all of these levels of relationships in order for us to be what we were created to be—His temple.

CHAPTER TWELVE

Leave, Cleave, and Become

The next verse in our study is Ephesians 5:31:

"For this cause a man shall leave his father and mother, and shall cleave to his wife; and the two shall become one flesh."

In-laws can be great blessings, but it is well known that some of the biggest problems in marriages can come from in-laws. Even so, I have never known in-laws who were causing major problems in a son or daughter's marriage who were not sincerely trying to help, and actually thought they were helping. Even in some ways they may have been helping, while in other ways they were causing major problems.

It is crucial for every young couple to develop their own family, and their own identity as a family. To have a healthy marriage we should not try to make our spouse into a reflection of a parent. We must learn to cleave to each other until we become one. To do this most couples really do need to **"leave"** their fathers and mothers, literally getting far enough away from them so as not to be interfered with. Of course few young couples want to hear this, and even fewer parents do, but it is usually essential for a healthy, lasting marriage.

This is not to imply that there should not be a relationship with our parents after we are married. However, our relationship to our parents must radically change after marriage. Even so, it is normal for parents to try to make their children into their own image, and to have a lasting relationship with them. Didn't God, our Father, make us in His image, and want to have a lasting relationship with us? It is therefore understandable that parents would want to do the same with their children. However, just as the Lord also made each of His children to be unique, and gave them remarkable freedom to develop their uniqueness, parents must do the same with their children.

We must especially give our children space during the first few years of their marriage. Each new family formed is also a new beginning in a way. They must be free to form their own special identity and uniqueness. Only then will they be strong enough to actually carry on the family name and good traditions which is right for them to do. Why is this?

There was a lot of talk a few years ago about the bondage of co-dependence and how to be free of it. In a popular book written on this subject it was acknowledged that the highest form of relationship was *interdependence*. However, the only way one could enter into this highest form of unity was to be delivered from co-dependence, which is where one does not have their own identity. To do this they had to go through the stage of independence until their own identity had been formed and made strong enough to have an interdependent relationship where their identity was not swallowed up and lost. There is an important truth to this.

Every infant is co-dependent. It cannot make it without its parents. As it grows it gradually becomes more self-sufficient and independent. This is a purpose of maturity, and if a child is maturing in a healthy way, it will become more independent. However, there is a difference between the independence of maturity and the independence of rebellion. Even so, parents who have best raised their children have raised them to the level of maturity where they do not need their parents. Then, once their independence is established and they have their own unique identity, the relationship between the parents and children can go on to the highest level of relationship, which is interdependence. This is where we can have a relationship but not try to consume each other's identity, but fully appreciate each other's uniqueness.

This is important to understand about marriage relationships, but Paul did not write this to the Ephesians about marriage relationships. As he goes on to say in the next verse, **"This mystery is great; but I am speaking with reference to Christ and the church" (Ephesians 5:32).** Paul was talking about the marriage between Christ and His church. This remains such a **"mystery"** to this day that many still do not comprehend, but it is becoming increasingly crucial that we do. So how does it apply?

In the story line of the Bible, the Father married Israel and together they had a Son. The Son was also to have a bride—the church. From the very beginning the mother, Israel, tried to impose herself on the young bride of Christ through the "Judaizers" who tried to bring her under the yoke of the Law. This was an attempt to make the young church completely co-dependent and swallow up her unique identity. If this had happened there would have been no New Covenant, and eventually all of the truth of the Messiah would have been swallowed up. There had to be a separation—a leaving until the church was able to establish her own identity with Christ, her husband.

The church has now gone through her independent stage, and though her marriage has been about as rocky as Israel's was with the Father, we are coming to the time of reconciliation, healing, and the ultimate union. It is no accident that as this is happening, there are still modern forms of the first century heresy trying to draw the church under the yoke of the Law and swallow her up in Judaism again. It will not succeed, but if it did it would completely jeopardize the very purpose of the church.

There is much controversy today about what is referred to as "replacement theology." This is the theology whereby the church completely replaces Israel in God's plan. All of the promises that were given to Israel are now really meant for the church. This is to some degree a reaction to Israel's attempts to destroy the unique identity of the church. Because of this the church has also gone through a long period, centuries, of trying to destroy the unique identity of Israel. Now, possibly in reaction to the replacement theology, there are "counter-replacement" theologies being promoted whereby Israel completely displaces the church in God's plan at the end. Both of these theologies are in error, and disregard major portions of Scripture in both the Old and New Testaments.

In the end there will be a unity in the entire family of God as we read about in Ephesians 2, with the enmity between Israel and the church being abolished. This will result in such a powerful union in the end that it will be called **"one new man" (Ephesians 2:15).** However, this will not come by either the church or Israel swallowing up the identity of the other, but by each becoming strong enough in their own identity to enter into the highest form of unity—interdependence.

This does not imply that Israel will establish its righteousness through the Law. Israel will acknowledge their Messiah, and the cross as the only remedy for sin and reconciliation with God. However, there was always intended to be a uniqueness between the Hebrew believers and the Gentile believers. This is why the Lord had an "apostle to the Jews" and an "apostle to the Gentiles," otherwise there would have been no need for such distinctions.

The way I become one with my wife is not by making her into a man, but by appreciating her uniqueness. The same kind of maturity will be required between the church and Israel so the ultimate unity can take place. This remains a mystery to most, but when we mature we will begin to understand it, and then enter into it.

CHAPTER THIRTEEN

Nevertheless

O ur next verse in our study is Ephesians 5:33:

"Nevertheless let each individual among you also love his own wife even as himself; and let the wife see to it that she respect her husband."

The first word in this verse is important, **"nevertheless."** In modern English it comes across as an expression of resignation, but this was not the case originally. It was formed from the combining of three words, NEVER-THE-LESS, and was a powerful exhortation not to choose the way which leads to "less." This is obviously the way the apostle meant it here. To paraphrase it he was saying something like, "If you really want the best out of life, and not the least, husbands love your wives as yourself, and wives respect your husbands." This is one factor which can determine if we are going to live our lives to the fullest, or settle for "less."

It is interesting here that the husbands are commanded to love their wives, but the wives are not commanded to love their husbands, but rather to respect them. This is because, as a generalization, women tend to need love more than respect, and men tend to need respect more than love. This does not mean women do not need respect, or men love, but the order of need tends to be different for men and women.

It is probably not an over-generalization to say that most people seem to think that most people think just like they do. However, people are so diverse and unique that this is almost never the case. Therefore, generalizations are never going to be completely accurate. However, because women may tend to need love first, it is likely they will assume that their husbands feel the same way, when it is not at all the case. Men, who in general may not need many displays of affection from their wives, may tend to feel that their wives feel the same, when they do not. The different degrees of need for affection and respect is one of the basic differences between men and women which the opposite sex has a difficult time understanding, and why the apostle gives this exhortation.

Personally, when my wife has in some way shown me disrespect, I feel that she is being hypocritical when she tries to make up with love and affection. However, she does not feel this way at all, but feels she is doing the right thing to bring reconciliation. She does not seem to even see the two as related. I have observed the same with my daughters, and other women I have worked with. The women generally seem far more concerned that I like them as people. They want to be esteemed for who they are, not just for their work. However, with my sons, or the men that I work with, it is obvious they are far more concerned that I respect them, and their work.

Paul's exhortation was for men to understand that our wives want us to notice more than just their work—they want us to notice and appreciate them! For the wives though, it may be hard to understand. Your husband probably cares more about that you respect his work, or his other accomplishments, even in such things as sports or hobbies, than he cares about being viewed personally. This does not mean he does not desire for you to be attracted to him and appreciate him personally, but that is likely going to be secondary to him.

So Paul's exhortation in this verse was a remarkably insightful attempt to help men and women build bridges across their differences. Men need to work at being affectionate, and women need to work at ways to show respect for their husbands and their work.

Now this is an extremely superficial treatment of a most profound subject. However, if we are going to go for God's highest, and "never-the-less," this is something that every husband and wife is going to have to work at.

Before we go on to the next part of this study we should also recognize it was after Paul gave the revelation of the glorious purpose of the church that he started his teaching on the family. We cannot become the church we are called to be without becoming the families that we are called to be.

This does not mean we should neglect the church until we get things right in our families. The church is one of the places we should be getting the most help for our family. Likewise, as leaders of churches in whatever capacity, we must keep in mind that if our families are not strong the church will not be strong, and it will fall short of what it is called to be. We must grow in our church life and our family life together.

PART VII

Prepared for All Things

A Study of Ephesians
Chapter 6

C H A P T E R   F O U R T E E N

The Beginning of Judgment

Our text for this chapter continues the emphasis on family relationships. Ephesians 6:1 states:

Children, obey your parents in the Lord, for this is right.

Children are exhorted to obey their parents for one reason—it is right. This one thing, children learning to obey their parents, is one of the most important factors in learning to discern right from wrong. Parents who are not helping them is one of the main reasons why terrible judgments will come upon the world in the last days, as the prophecies in Scripture make clear. One of the greatest evils to come upon the earth in the last days is lawlessness. Learning to respect and obey authority is one of the greatest foundations we can lay in our children's lives to prepare them to combat this.

The first word given to Samuel the prophet by the Lord should be a most sobering exhortation to every parent. This is recorded in I Samuel 3:11-14:

And the LORD said to Samuel, "Behold, I am about to do a thing in Israel at which both ears of everyone who hears it will tingle.

In that day I will carry out against Eli all that I have spoken concerning his house, from beginning to end.

For I have told him that I am about to judge his house forever for the iniquity which he knew, because his sons brought a curse on themselves and he did not rebuke them.

And therefore I have sworn to the house of Eli that the iniquity of Eli's house shall not be atoned for by sacrifice or offering forever."

When the Lord said that this was going to be something He would do to make the ears of all who heard it tingle, He meant for it to wake up every one in Israel. The seriousness of this matter could not be overstated. Our ears should also burn at this most sobering rebuke. The sin of letting our children bring a curse on themselves without correcting them is so serious the Lord declares that it **"shall not be atoned for by sacrifice or offering forever."**

A terrible judgment came upon Eli and his house just as was prophesied. We are told the Lord prefers mercy over judgment, and the Scriptures abundantly testify of His great patience with us. Whenever the Lord brought judgment, it was because of the serious and repeated violations of His standards and command-ments, which resulted in the corruption of the entire nation. God's eternal standards have never changed, and for these same reasons the Lord will bring judgment upon the whole world at the end. Today this "sin of Eli" is hastening the judgment of God because of the lawlessness it is releasing.

Eli was the high priest, and if he did not live by the highest standards it would lower the standards of the entire nation. Every Christian is likewise a priest and called to be the light and salt of the earth. When we do not live up to the highest standards, we too allow a tragic corruption in the nations that we have been sent to. This is also why it is required of all who serve in positions of authority in the church to keep their own children under control.

Of course this does not mean that those who are going to be leaders in the church must have perfect children. No one could ever serve as an authority in the church if that were the requirement. Many of the Lord's children fall into sin, rebel, and make a host of mistakes. We should also note that this has to do with children, not youth, or young adults. The children of leaders should be under very good control (and there is a "good" control). However, as our children get older they should be given more authority and responsibility, just as the Lord does with His children. Often even the best parents may see their children go astray for a while, just as the Lord's often do, but we should not blame the parent. Let's keep this verse relating to children.

It is noteworthy that Eli loved the Lord and the service of His tabernacle very much. In fact, he loved them so much, when the Ark of the Covenant was captured by the Philistines, he fell over and died. Eli did not mishandle the sacrifices, or do any of the other despicable things his sons did, yet he too was punished because of what they did. His punishment was so serious, no amount of sacrifices or offerings could atone for his sin—forever.

Now we may think, "Didn't Eli's sons do this when they were adults?" How does this relate to what was just said about this relating to children? For one thing, Eli's sons were serving as priests of the Lord with him. Priests were required to live by much higher standards than the other people in the Old Testament, just like the leadership in the New Testament are required to live by higher standards, as the qualifications make clear. Eli should have corrected his sons because their failures in the priesthood ultimately affected the whole nation. There are many examples of those in ministry whose natural children work with them and are allowed to get away with things they should not. Likewise, this will damage the whole church if not corrected. The standards set must relate to everyone, whether they are our children or not.

Also, this rebuke from the Lord given through Samuel to Eli did not mean that Eli could not be forgiven. What this meant was that all of his sacrifices and offerings could not atone for his irresponsibility with regard to his family. Many are likewise zealous for the Lord and His work as an attempt to atone for sin or irresponsibility in other areas of their lives. All of our zeal and good works will never atone for our sin. However, there was a sacrifice made through which we can be forgiven—the cross. Even so, we are not turning to the cross for forgiveness if we are still attempting to atone for our irresponsibility with our own works, as Eli was doing.

Even though we can be forgiven if we go to the cross of Jesus, the best answer to this problem is to *not need* forgiveness, because we are teaching our children obedience. This is not just for our sake, but also for the sake of our children and of the world to which we have been sent to be a light and salt. It is for this reason that we are told in I Peter 4:17:

> **"For it is time for judgment to begin with the household of God; and if it begins with us first, what will be the outcome for those who do not obey the gospel of God?"**

How could the Lord judge the world for these things if His own people were guilty? How could the Lord rebuke Eli if He were not going to discipline His children for these things? We can fully expect the Lord to deal with the church's lawlessness, the failure to discipline our children, and our other failures which have released the evil for which He is going to judge the world.

Eli was the high priest and still this came upon him. It does not matter how high we have risen in ministry—this same judgment will come upon us if we are not obedient to the most basic responsibilities given to us with our families. It does not matter how many mission trips we have been on, or how faithfully we have paid our tithes, if we do not raise our children right we will be in serious jeopardy.

James 5:12 states, **"...let your yes be yes, and your no, no; so that you may not fall under judgment."** This is one of the primary ways we can fall under judgment—when we do not mean what we say. When we say "yes" we should mean it, and stick to it. Likewise, when we say "no" that should be exactly what we mean.

What does this have to do with raising our children? When we tell them "yes" they should be taught that this is exactly what we mean. When we tell them "no," it should mean no the first time we say it. We should not have to repeat it over and over because our "yes" means "yes" and our "no" means "no." Some children are taught that their parents really do not mean what they say until they raise their voice to a certain decibel level. Is that a good way to teach them to hear the **"still small voice"** which the Lord often uses when speaking to us? When we say one thing, but our kids can pressure us into changing it, we are not teaching them right and wrong—we are teaching them to be manipulative and to disrespect authority.

Throughout Western society today there is an unrelenting assault on authority. There is hardly a sitcom on television today which does not seem to be designed to systematically erode people's respect for authority. They seem especially designed to be insulting to fathers, who in almost every sitcom are bungling idiots, constantly having to be rescued by their wives or children. Most sitcoms are just about as devoted to attacking moral values. This lawlessness which is being released will ultimately be a bigger threat to us than any enemy from without. If we are going to be the light and salt we are called to be, it will begin with how we teach our children.

CHAPTER FIFTEEN

The Beginning of Honor

We continue our study in this chapter with Ephesians 6:2-3:

"Honor your father and mother (which is the first commandment with a promise), that it may be well with you, and that you may live long on the earth."

Our verse for the last chapter was an exhortation for children to obey their parents in the Lord. Our verse for this chapter takes this further. It is one thing to obey someone, but it can be an entirely different matter to honor them. We can obey for many different reasons, some of which are selfish, or even with an evil intent of manipulation. However, when we honor the one we are obeying, it purifies the motives.

We also understand that honoring our fathers and mothers is simply the right thing to do. The Lord so esteems this that it is the only one of His commandments which carries a promise or a reward with it. If we do this we are promised that it will be well with us, and we will live long on the earth. This is so important to the Lord because it is one of the primary foundations in our lives which will help us to resist the spirit of lawlessness that is growing, and will ultimately bring much destruction upon the world. It is for a good reason that the anti-Christ, who brings such destruction, is called **"the man of lawlessness,"** or **"the lawless one."**

In our verse for the last chapter, children are commanded to obey their parents **"in the Lord,"** which many have interpreted to be our spiritual parents. It is obviously both, our natural and spiritual parents, but as we largely addressed our earthly family relationships in the last chapter, let us look at our spiritual relationships now.

One reason many churches and movements do not last long is because they fail to honor their spiritual parents. They dishonor them by seeking to point out their flaws and mistakes. Flaws and mistakes do not need to be covered up, but when we uncover them disrespectfully, in order to make ourselves look better, we will not last long on the earth. This mentality does affect many, compelling them to spend a great deal of effort trying not to be like their parents. Because of this unrighteous judgment, they inevitably do become like their parents, and often end up making even greater mistakes.

From the perspective of church history, we can see a certain, definite spiritual progression with each new, spiritual generation. However, we could never have gone as far if it were not for those who went before us making the progress they did. We must always keep this in mind, and respect our fathers and mothers in the Lord who have given us so much.

One of the ways the children of Israel honored their fathers and mothers was to drink from the wells they had dug. I think we can do this by reading and honoring the teachings of our spiritual parents who went before us. This is one reason why I spend so much of my time reading church history and the works of those who had a great impact on the church.

I also think one of our greatest failures is honoring our spiritual fathers without honoring our spiritual mothers. There are many great women of God whose contributions to the church were extraordinary, and yet they are rarely mentioned. It is by honoring both fathers *and* mothers that the promise is given that it will go well with us, and we will live long on the earth. It is good to honor our fathers and mothers in history, but it is even more important to honor the spiritual fathers and mothers who are still with us.

It is interesting how, as the Lord Jesus remarked, the Pharisees loved to honor the tombs of the prophets, while resisting the greatest prophet of all, who was with them. It is much easier to honor those who are now dead and can no longer be a threat to us, than those who are commanding our obedience now. As Francis Frangipane once pointed out, "It is a religious spirit that gives honor to what God has done while resisting what He is doing."

What can you do to honor your natural father and mother? Likewise, what can you do to honor your spiritual father and mother? Why not take at least one service a year to teach on the great things the founders of your denomination, movement, or church did and taught? If your natural parents are still alive, why not have them come at least once a year to honor them in a special way?

These are just a couple of ideas, but my point is that this is not a passive matter. If we are going to combat the emerging spirit of lawlessness, we must actively resist it by obeying these exhortations of Scripture.

CHAPTER SIXTEEN

The Instruction of the Lord

We continue our study in this chapter with Ephesians 6:4:

And, fathers, do not provoke your children to anger; but bring them up in the discipline and instruction of the Lord.

It is noteworthy that this exhortation is to fathers instead of mothers. It is not always the case, but usually fathers are the main disciplinarians in the family. Mothers tend to be more nurturing, and prone to mercy. Fathers can be more prone to anger, which can cause them to carry discipline too far. Discipline not carried far enough can result in rebellion, and discipline carried too far can also result in rebellion in our children, provoking them to anger instead of obedience from the heart.

It is also noteworthy that the apostle's instruction for how to not provoke our children to anger is to bring them up in the discipline and instruction of the Lord. The Lord loves all people, but seems to have a special love for children. He included an abundance of wisdom in His Word for how to raise them and take care of them. One of the foundations of this **"discipline and instruction of the Lord"** is consistency. One of the basic characteristics of the Lord's nature is that He is consistent, and therefore, His discipline and instruction will be consistent.

As stated before, we have probably all witnessed parents who must tell their children "no" repeatedly, usually raising their voices or threatening them, before their children believe they really mean "no." If we are going to raise our children in the discipline and admonition of the Lord, we must teach them that our "yes" means "yes" and our "no" means "no" the first time we say it. Neither should we have to raise our voices to them, since a basic characteristic of the way the Lord speaks to us is in a **"still small voice."**

Also, if we have taught our children that they don't have to obey us until we raise our voices, they learn we don't mean what we say until there is a certain level of frustration on our part. Only the Spirit can beget that which is Spirit, and only discipline given in the Spirit of the Lord will bring forth the fruit of the Spirit. Frustration is not a fruit of the Spirit.

You may wonder if it is possible to discipline our children in the Spirit—not only is it possible, it is the only way we should discipline them. All discipline should be done in love for their sakes, and not because we are frustrated with them. If you have to discipline them for something which has made you angry, wait until you have control of your anger before you discipline them.

Regardless of what the humanists declare, spanking is the most effective form of discipline for younger children. As Proverbs 13:24 states, **"He who spares his rod hates his son, but he who loves him disciplines him diligently."** The first point is that if we really love our children, we will discipline them diligently. This is Christlikeness, as we are told in Hebrews 12:5-6, **"... My son, do not regard lightly the discipline of the Lord, nor faint when you are reproved by Him; for those whom the Lord loves He disciplines, and He scourges every son whom He receives."**

Because of the prevalence of humanistic philosophies which are contrary to the Word of God, many have come to perceive discipline as rejection, when the opposite is true. The scariest thing in the world is to be allowed to get away with things for which we should be disciplined. We should take the correction and discipline which we receive from the Lord as proof of His love. Our children should do the same when they receive our correction and discipline. If they have been disciplined rightly, they will. It will give them great security knowing you love them enough to discipline them.

Humanistic teachings on child rearing have tried to make parents feel guilty about spanking their children, saying it is violence and imparts violence to children. The opposite is actually the truth, as is usually the case with humanistic philosophies. I personally think the Lord put some extra padding back there so children could be spanked in a way that would cause some pain, but no injury. Spanking resolves the conflict and gets the discipline over fast, which is much more merciful than dragging the issue out with other popular forms, such as time outs or taking away privileges. These are not necessarily wrong, but we need to consider that the biblical exhortations on how to discipline are always going to be the best.

When I spank my younger children, I try to be sure that I am over any anger which I had as a result of their offense. I sit with them and talk to them about why I must discipline them. Then I try to spank them consistently, using about the same number of whacks for each offense. I then sit and hold them until they stop crying and tell them that they are forgiven. We pray and ask God's forgiveness, and then I will play with them, tickle them, or do something until we are laughing together and I am sure that there has been total reconciliation and forgiveness with no continuing rift between us.

We also need to understand that the word "discipline" does not necessarily mean punishment, but rather the training of a disciple. If we had enough positive training we probably would not have to do as much punishing for offenses.

In all of this we must keep in mind that our first command is to love our children. I personally believe that we should be giving our children ten times as much love and "positive time" as discipline. Therefore, when one of my children is going through an especially difficult time, it is even more important to give that child a lot of positive attention and love. Discipline is important, but love is our most powerful weapon. True love entails discipline, but it must always be done in love.

CHAPTER SEVENTEEN

The Freedom
of Slavery

We continue our study in this chapter with Ephesians 6:5-6:

Slaves, be obedient to those who are your masters according to the flesh, with fear and trembling, in the sincerity of your heart, as to Christ;

not by way of eyeservice, as men-pleasers, but as slaves of Christ, doing the will of God from the heart.

Many wonder why the Scriptures do not directly condemn some of the great social evils such as slavery and abortion. The historian, Will Durant, articulated this well when he said, "Caesar sought to change men by changing institutions. Jesus changed institutions by changing men."

We see an example of this in the book of Philemon. In this letter, Paul admonishes a slave owner, whom he had personally led to the Lord, to receive his runaway slave back, **"no longer as a slave, but more than a slave, a beloved brother"** (verse 16). Any believer who is growing in Christ will be convicted by abusing or mistreating his fellow man, or by not paying the laborer his worthy wages. In this way, not only slavery, but all forms of oppression and wrong treatment of others are addressed.

There are people who may be wealthy and have many working for them, but they are bound and oppressed if they are slaves to their wealth. In Christ, you can be very poor in relation to the world's wealth, and yet be freer and happier than the wealthiest person. In Christ even a slave or a prisoner can be the most free person on earth.

It is much better to be free spiritually and be a slave in the natural than free in the natural but a slave in spirit. However, the best is to be free in all things. There is no question that the Lord wants this for all people. Freedom is so important to the Lord that we are told in II Corinthians 3:17, **"...where the Spirit of the Lord is, there is liberty."**

One of the most oppressive yokes of bondage is the "fear of man." Under this one yoke comes other fears such as the fear of rejection, failure, etc. Therefore, one of the most basic ways we can free ourselves of this terrible yoke is simply to do what we do for the Lord rather than for men. Of course, one of the most debilitating and self-destructive forms of the fear of man is to practice our religion before men. The Lord makes clear in Matthew 6 that this is the foundation of a hypocritical life.

It is also true that when we start doing our work as unto the Lord we can turn the worst drudgery into worship and experience the pleasure of the Lord in it. And when we do our work as unto the Lord we can be joined to Him in His yoke, which means that we therefore will be aided by His strength. Fellowship with Him in the worst job will be better than even the best job without Him. This is true freedom.

Now let us look at the next verses in our study, Ephesians 6:7-8:

> **With good will render service, as to the Lord, and not to men,**
>
> **knowing that whatever good thing each one does, this he will receive back from the Lord, whether slave or free.**

Again, to do what we do as unto the Lord, not men, is the source of the greatest liberty we can ever know. If we are true slaves of Christ, there is no yoke that man can ever put on us.

Also, the slave owner is responsible for the well being of his slaves. If we have given our lives to the Lord to serve Him, we can trust Him to accomplish all things for our good. For this reason, we must also accept every job as from Him, and do every job as unto Him—with all of our hearts, as all service to the King deserves. If we do this we are promised that we will receive back from the Lord, which is to say, we also look to the Lord as the One who rewards us, not the paymaster.

Many people live from payday to payday. They have the mentality that if they could just get a big enough raise, all their troubles would be over. The truth is most of us do not need more money. If we made more money we would soon be in the same situation because we would spend more. Others just need to have "the devourer rebuked," the one who causes the constant problems and breakdowns, resulting in extra expenses. Regardless of which it is, or whether it is both, it is faith that releases the hand of God in our lives. When we go to work every day with the mentality that we work for the Lord, not just the company, it begins to release the faith which will move God on our behalf.

The Scriptures are full of the promises of rewards from God. Some we receive in eternity, but many we are promised for this life. In eternity we will experience joy that is beyond our present ability to comprehend. But one of the great promises the obedient can have is to begin to experience the joy of the Lord now, as we are told in Psalm 16:11, **"Thou wilt make known to me the path of life; in Thy presence is fulness of joy; in Thy right hand there are pleasures forever."**

The rewards of serving the Lord which we receive in this life are more than worth it. We will never receive better wages for anything than what we do for the Lord. Even so, what we receive here is only the small down payment for rewards that are much greater, which will last forever. There is no better employer in the universe than our God. However, the greatest joy of all is not in what we get, but in beholding the joy which He receives from us. Think about that. You can bring joy to God Almighty!

Your devotion to the Lord in the midst of such darkness and hardship can touch Him deeply. It is even a witness to principalities and powers. For us there will be no greater joy than to see on His face in that great day the joy He has received from our obedience and devotion.

The first two modern missionaries were sent out from the Moravian community at Herrnhut, Germany located on the estate of Count Zinzendorf. To pay their passage to the West Indies to preach to the slaves there, they sold themselves as indentured servants—they became slaves to reach the slaves. One of them was betrothed to be married. As the ship they were taking pulled away from the dock, his fiancée, who knew that she would never see him alive again, cried out, "Why, why would you do this?" His answer was simply, "So that the Savior can receive the reward of His sacrifice." He was not even thinking of his own reward, which certainly must be great, but rather he was thinking of how the Savior deserved His reward—the souls of those for which He gave His life.

Certainly our rewards for service to Him will be beyond our present ability to comprehend, but what will be greater than seeing Him receive His reward? It is not wrong to work for our rewards. In fact, the Lord Himself did this as it says in Hebrews 12:2, "**...who for the joy set before Him endured the cross, despising the shame, and has sat down at the right hand of the throne of God.**" However, without question, our greatest reward of all will be to see the joy that our obedience, faith, and worship have brought to Him. The greatest joy of all creation will be seeing the Savior receive the reward of His sacrifice.

CHAPTER EIGHTEEN

Give Up Threatening

I n this chapter, we will go to our next verse, Ephesians 6:9:

And, masters, do the same things to them, and give up threatening, knowing that both their Master and yours is in heaven, and there is no partiality with Him.

Of course this is a continuation of the theme which exhorted slaves to do their work as unto the Lord and not unto men. **"Do the same things"** means that the masters should also do their work as unto the Lord. How could the master of slaves do that? As the verse continues, it is by knowing that the true Master is in heaven, which means that those who are in their charge are His servants, not theirs.

This one verse, if observed, might have so revolutionized slavery that it would have been a much more humane institution. It still does not mean that slavery was right, and that it would not have needed to be abolished. As we studied previously, it is much better to be free, and freedom is a basic goal of Christianity for every person. Even so, how would the above verse have revolutionized slavery, and how does this apply to us today?

Let's think about how we would act if we lived in a kingdom where the king put us in charge of his own personal servants. Would we not treat his servants with the utmost dignity and respect? Would we not be devoted to their health and well being, knowing the king would hold us responsible? This is what the apostle was trying to convey to the slave owners of his time, that the true Master of the slaves in their charge was also their Master—they were all slaves of Christ regardless of their position on earth. In this way the earthly masters were to lead their slaves as unto the Lord, for the Lord's purposes and not just their own.

It is interesting that the apostle also commands the slave owners to **"give up threatening."** Threatening is demeaning and should never be exercised by anyone in authority. We should have clear guidelines, with rewards for good behavior and penalties for bad behavior, just as the Lord Himself established both in the Old and New Covenants. When the Lord stated the penalty for disobedience, it was not as a threat, but the warning of a sure result. For Him to just go on threatening without keeping His word in these matters would have only caused all to lose respect for Him and His Word. The same happens to us when we resort to threatening instead of keeping our word.

When we threaten our children or employees, it is the evidence of a lack of true authority. The rewards and penalties should already be clear, and if there is disobedience, there should be discipline the first time, not further threatening. If we have to threaten in order to compel our children or anyone else that we are in charge of to obey us, then somehow it has already been established that our "yes" does not really mean "yes," and our "no" does not really mean "no."

In whatever capacity we find ourselves as leaders, we need to keep in mind that we are under the leadership of the King. Even as parents, our children are not our children. They are His and He has given us the supreme privilege and responsibility of raising and watching over them. If we are employers, supervisors, or are in any way in authority over others, we must always keep in mind that these are the Lord's people, which we have been given the responsibility to lead. We must always do this with the utmost respect for them, and the authority which we have been trusted with. This should compel us to keep our word in all things and in all ways if at all possible. When we start threatening instead of enforcing, there has been an erosion of authority and respect, and this will hurt everyone.

Over the years, I have had to lay off a few people who worked for our ministry for either substandard performance, or for seriously violating the policies and regulations which govern our ministry. This is the hardest thing I have to do as a leader of our ministry. In almost every case, the people leave hurt and angry regardless of how I try to make it easier by commending them for the good things they did, etc. I can still remember the looks on the faces of every one who I have had to lay off when I told them. Several said, "I never thought you would do this!" Two of these actually said that they never thought that I would do it because no one in their life had ever enforced such a standard. However, several of these sought me out later, some years later, to tell me that my firing them was the best thing that had happened to them. Each of these have gone on to unprecedented success, which they attributed to the wake up of their firing or layoff. Of course, this has not been the case with all. Some became bitter instead of better, and I can't help that.

I am not trying to make excuses for these people or their problems. But when we fail to do what we say, and instead resort to threatening, or pressuring people to do what we say in place of our "yes" meaning "yes" and our "no" meaning "no," we are hurting them far more than they will be hurt by our discipline. To repeat, one of the ultimate evils released in the last days is lawlessness. And the lack of true authority which functions with dignity and respect for those in our charge, is helping to release this ultimate evil. If we are going to be an authority who represents the King of kings, our word must be true.

CHAPTER NINETEEN

Be Strong in the Lord

O ur verse for this chapter is Ephesians 6:10:

Finally, be strong in the Lord, and in the strength of His might.

When the apostle writes **"finally"** here it means that this begins the concluding thought to the entire Epistle. For a letter which is so rich and deep in the revelation of the glory and purpose of the church, we can be sure the conclusion is going to be a powerful one and we are not disappointed. In the last few sentences, we are told if everything he has written about is to be fulfilled, it will be by **"the strength of His might."**

This one issue is what makes Christianity so revolutionary and so powerful. For other religions, the main issue is how many can become righteous enough and do enough good works to be accepted by God. Of course, this promotes self-righteousness. True, biblical Christianity is the exact opposite of this vain pursuit which drives every religion. This is not to say we do not have good works, but our righteousness is provided for us through the cross of Jesus. He then strengthens us to stand in this righteousness and do the good works that we are called to do.

Because our devotion as Christians is not just to better ourselves, but to pursue the righteousness and strength of the Lord, we should have no foundation for becoming proud and self-righteous, both of which are roots of the fall and of man's ultimate failure. This fundamental issue of pursuing the righteousness and strength of the Lord will keep us on the path of life if we do not lose focus on it. Even the works we do are done in His strength, and it casts us in total dependence on the Lord. Without Him, we have nothing.

This is a truth which becomes more and more clear as we mature in Christ. It causes us not only to become even more attached to Him, but more focused on Him instead of on ourselves. As we do this, and behold His glory, we are changed into His same image, and this is the ultimate goal of our faith.

We cannot accomplish one thing of eternal value in our own strength. The more we come to realize this, the more power we can be trusted with. What could we do with the strength of His might? What would we do? These are questions we should be asking.

What could we do? Anything. I oversee a diverse ministry that is really like eight separate ministries. I often feel I could devote all of my time and energy to just one of these and it still would not be enough. At times the administrative responsibilities seem more than any human could handle. One day as I was especially under the weight of this, the Lord spoke to me and said, "I can help you with that. After all, I uphold the universe with My power."

So I asked the Lord for the ability to accomplish in minutes what often took me many hours to do. He immediately began to answer this prayer. I asked for the gift of a word of wisdom to be able to see right to the heart of a matter, and to know what to do without having to take hours to study and research it. He gave it to me. Some of our ministry departments were more than an hour and a half away so I was rarely able to visit them. But the Lord would give me insight into bottlenecks, or other problems, and I would go there and find it as I had seen, and know exactly what to do about the problems. Before, such problems would take many days just to unravel and fix. Now they only take minutes. This one thing began to radically change my life. I began to actually have free time again.

This is not to imply that I do all of this perfectly, or that there are not times when issues take longer. One of the primary ways the Lord has helped me to carry these responsibilities is to give me some of the best co-laborers as department heads and managers. However, this pursuit of knowing the Lord's strength in carrying administrative responsibilities has relieved the constant heavy burden I carried for so long, and has turned it into a joy and excitement. I honestly never thought this could happen, but it has.

This is but a small example of how we are to learn to rely on His strength and power. Ultimately, we should seek to do everything in His strength. Think about that. It will lead to a life of miracles. That may sound fantastic, but it is our calling, and is supposed to be normal Christianity. The Lord said that if we had just the faith of a mustard seed, we could move mountains. What mountains are in your life which you need to have moved? The Lord hung the sun, the moon, and the stars—a mountain is a small thing for Him. He can lift all of our mountains together and not even break a sweat! This one thing, being **"strong in the Lord and in the strength of His might"** can turn any life of burden and drudgery into one of such accomplishments that all will know without a doubt that God is with you.

We should look to Him with any part of our lives that seems overwhelming and beyond our control—that we might know Him and **"the strength of His might."**

CHAPTER TWENTY

God's Armor

Right after the exhortation to **"be strong in the Lord and in the strength of His might,"** we are given a most curious exhortation in the next verse, Ephesians 6:11:

> **Put on the full armor of God, that you may be able to stand firm against the schemes of the devil.**

If we can live in the strength of the Lord's might, why do we need armor? This is one of the ways He gives us His strength and might. Every piece of this armor is a spiritual aspect of His nature, and of what He is doing through His people on the earth, which we will see as we continue this study.

The first point is that we must put on spiritual armor. The next one is that we must put on the *"full armor of God,"* not just part of it. If we leave any of it off, we can be sure the devil will hit us right in that place.

We do not find a single place in the Scripture where it tells us that we can take this armor off. We live in enemy territory. We have been dropped behind enemy lines. As we are told in I John 5:19, **"We know that we are of God, and the whole world lies in the power of the evil one."** When you are in the middle of a war, you cannot just ask the enemy to stop shooting so you can rest for a while. This life is going to be a battle! Even so, battles are opportunities for victory. Instead of trying to avoid conflict, we must learn to recognize them as the opportunities that they are, and seize them.

This does not mean we can never know times of rest and peace. In fact, one of the greatest weapons that we have been given against the power of the devil is the peace of God. However, this peace is not the cessation of any conflict in our lives, but it is a peace that we experience even in the midst of the greatest battle. Even though we can know the greatest peace in even the greatest battle, there is no time we should ever let our guard down or take our armor off. However, there will be times in our lives when we are not engaged in a specific battle.

The third point is that this armor is the **"armor of God,"** not just protection we have come up with ourselves. We can be sure this is a protection that will certainly withstand any attack of the enemy. It will fully protect us in this life, and if we have been obedient, we can expect this protection from any weapon that is formed against us.

How would your life be different if you had a visit from Michael, the archangel, and he gave you a special suit that would protect you from any harm that could ever come to you? You could do anything and never be injured. We have been given just such a suit! It did not come from Michael the archangel, but from God! It is a suit that is provided for every Christian. You can put on this suit and be fully protected from any harm which even the devil himself would try to do to you.

The next point is that this armor is given to us so we can **"stand firm."** It seems this armor only covers our fronts, not our backs, implying that if we turn and run there is no protection and the enemy will be able to get his shots in. Once we embrace the truth of the gospel, we must set our faces like flint and determine to go forward in our pursuit of God and His truth, and to never retreat before the enemies of the cross.

The fact that the armor does not cover our backs also implies we will need other believers to watch our backs. You cannot watch someone else's back if you are busy watching your own.

If we try to watch our own backs, we will always be looking in the wrong direction, so we must trust others to do this for us. The Lord has composed His body so that we will need each other.

The last point is that this armor is given to us so we can stand against the **"schemes"** of the devil, not just against his weapons. The devil will rarely attack someone directly, but will sneak around to find a position from which he can get a shot in. The devil is not a fair fighter. He cares nothing at all about "rules of engagement." In fact, we can count on him to break every rule if it will give him an edge. One of his most effective schemes is to get us to start breaking the rules in order to counter him. We don't need to do anything but put the full armor of God on and we will be able to stand against any scheme he has. This is what we will be covering in the next few chapters.

CHAPTER TWENTY-ONE

The Struggle

In our next verse, before Paul begins to explain the armor of God that we have been given, he explains a little bit about the conflict in Ephesians 6:12:

> **For our struggle is not against flesh and blood, but against the rulers, against the powers, against the world forces of this darkness, against the spiritual forces of wickedness in the heavenly places.**

The first point in this verse is that we are not fighting **"flesh and blood,"** or other people. The devil uses people, other Christians, and even us at times. If we see the real conflict, we will therefore not get angry with or try to fight other people, but rather the forces which seek to control them. It is a major victory for us to help free the person to which the devil has gained such access.

The next point is that we must recognize our fight is against **"rulers, powers, world forces of this darkness, and spiritual forces of wickedness."** Who would have thought that little, old me would be so important? If you are a born again Christian, little, old you has the power of the One who created the universe living in you. If you were ever to get completely free, fully believing God to release His power through you, you would be the greatest threat to the devil on the earth. You don't have to go to seminary to do this, and you don't have to have decades of experience. You simply have to believe God. This belief comes as we stop looking at ourselves and our shortcomings, and start looking at God and His strength.

The Greek word translated **"struggle"** in this verse is sometimes translated "wrestle." Wrestling is the closest form of combat. It is a face to face encounter. I know many people who try to cast down principalities and powers with prayer, but I have never seen it work. You can cast out demons, but you must wrestle down principalities. This type of wrestling requires going face to face with it where it is manifested. This is why we see in Luke 10 when the Lord sent the seventy out to preach the gospel, they came back excited that the demons were subject to them. But the Lord said something even greater had happened—He had seen Satan himself fall from heaven! Apostolic preaching is required to displace the devil—the light must go forth to cast out the darkness.

This "wrestling," or **"struggle"** against principalities can take on many forms, depending on how deeply the devil has taken over a place. For example, if he has taken over the courts, you may find yourself battling in the courts. If he has taken over the government, you will have a struggle there. Even so, in each of these places, the truth must be spoken, and the light must go forth from those who walk in the light to displace the darkness. This is why Paul the apostle had to be tried by his own nation so he could stand for truth there, going all the way to Caesar to testify of the truth at the highest levels.

We may think this did not accomplish much since Paul was eventually executed for his testimony, but it did accomplish much in the heavenly realm. It actually began to unravel the evil one's power over the Roman Empire so that the gospel would spread more readily throughout it. We too may appear in court and lose the case, but if we have stood for truth and declare it, we probably will accomplish much more than we can see from our perspective, just as the seventy did in Luke 10.

To really understand what is being accomplished by our lives, and our message, the "eyes of our hearts" must be opened just as the apostle Paul prayed at the beginning of this Epistle. We also need to keep in mind that we are not wrestling with flesh and blood, and not to keep looking at what is going on at that level. If we get the victory in the heavenly realm, it will eventually result in people getting free, but we must keep our attention on where the fight is.

We also must keep in mind that we are not to war according to our own strength, but in the **"strength of His might,"** or by God's strength and power. Therefore, our primary strategy in all spiritual warfare is not just to come up with a more brilliant strategy. The devil has been around for thousands of years and is much smarter than we are to begin with. We are not going to outsmart him. Neither do we need to be overly concerned about what the devil is doing. Effective spiritual warfare is not devil-centered but God-centered. Our goal is not to be more brilliant, but to be more obedient so that we more fully abide in Him. The more perfectly we abide in Him, the more of His strength and power we will have. Remember we only have true spiritual authority to the degree we are abiding in the King.

Our next verse, Ephesians 6:13, reiterates many of the things that the apostle has already said:

> **Therefore, take up the full armor of God, that you may be able to resist in the evil day, and having done everything, to stand firm.**

As a famous Bible teacher once said, "every time you see a 'therefore' written, you should go back and see what it is *there for.*" In this verse, we see that the **"therefore"** is a reference to the nature of our struggle with principalities and powers referred to in the previous verse. This is also a repetition of the command in verse 11 to **"put on the full armor of God."** Anytime something is repeated in Scripture, we should understand it is because of the increased importance of what is being said. If the apostle thought this was so important to repeat it so quickly, then we too should take the time to review the exhortation, which we will do, with the added insights the verse gives.

We are in a battle which we will be in throughout our lives on this earth. Until the kingdom comes so that authority over the earth is restored to God, we are living in enemy territory. If we do not put on the armor which God has provided for us on our mission here, we can expect continual wounding, which is precisely what many believers endure for their entire lives, and could have avoided. We have a simple choice. What are we going to do about it? I think that only the most foolish would not endeavor to learn how to put on the armor which has been provided for us. This we intend to do as we study the subsequent verses.

The apostle also repeats the exhortation to **"stand,"** only adding the addendum **"firm."** For all soldiers of the cross there must be a commitment from the very beginning that we will never compromise our convictions and we will never retreat before the enemies of the cross. We will stand firm regardless of the consequences. Retreat is not an option for us.

As we read in Proverbs 28:1, **"The wicked man flees though no one pursues, but the righteous are as bold as a lion"** (NIV). One of the primary characteristics found in every great man or woman of God in Scripture or history is their boldness in standing for truth and righteousness. What would our lives register on the "Boldness Scale" in standing for the truth of the gospel?

This is one reason we are told in Hebrews 11:6, **"And without faith it is impossible to please God, because anyone who comes to him must believe that he exists and that he rewards those who earnestly seek him"** (NIV). If we really believe in God, and believe that we have been entrusted with His truth, how can we fail to be bold with it? How can we be intimidated by pseudo-intellectuals or other enemies of the truth if we know the Lord? Every true believer will have a boldness and confidence that is uncommon in the world because we know the power, authority, and truth of the One we serve.

One reason many lose their boldness is because they allow the enemy to draw them into a fight on his grounds. One of the highest priorities of any general in warfare is to choose the field of battle. There are some who are equipped by God to fight on different fields. There are those who are equipped to fight on the field of philosophy or science, or to confront witchcraft, etc. One basic wisdom we need to operate under is to refuse to be drawn into battles that are outside of our realm of authority unless we have a special commission from the Lord, which will include a special grace for the purpose.

Even though we may refuse to be drawn into a fight for certain grounds where we are not equipped to fight on, this does not mean that we should ever retreat. In those cases, we still take our stand and refuse to give any of our ground to the enemy. Regardless of how the enemy attacks us, any retreat on our part could only come from a lack of faith in the One we serve. This is why the truly righteous, who are the ones with true faith, will always be as bold as lions. And this is why we are told in II Corinthians 3:12, **"Therefore, since we have such a hope, we are very bold"** (NIV).

As Christians we have a great advantage in this life. We can also go to the end of the book and read the end of the story—we win! As we are promised in II Corinthians 2:14, **"But thanks be to God, who always leads us in His triumph in Christ..."** If you were called upon to do something and were told that you absolutely could not fail, you could be quite bold in it, couldn't you? We have been promised success in this life, and a victory which will last forever! How can we fail to be bold with such a promise from none other than God Himself? This is why those who have true faith in God will stand and not compromise their convictions under any amount of pressure that the devil can bring upon them. The devil will test us, but those who really believe will always stand.

CHAPTER TWENTY-TWO

The Armor of Truth
and Righteousness

In this chapter we will begin our study of the armor of God in Ephesians 6:14:

Stand firm therefore, HAVING GIRDED YOUR LOINS WITH TRUTH

This is the third time in only four verses that Paul has said, **"stand,"** or **"stand firm."** He repeats this because it is essential for a victorious Christian life. We must be resolved that we will not be pushed back, we will not retreat, and we will not give up any ground to the enemy.

As we are told in James 4:7, **"Submit therefore to God. Resist the devil and he will flee from you."** Resisting is fighting, refusing to give ground. We must do this for the truth that has been entrusted to us. If we do this, the enemy will not just leave us alone, he will flee!

In explaining how to put on the armor of God, Paul begins by telling us to gird our loins with truth. **"Loins"** in Scripture is often used in reference to reproduction. To **"gird your loins"** is to clothe yourself in a way which your reproductive organs are protected. Of course this is speaking spiritually. So how do we gird our loins with truth?

First, it was considered a curse in biblical times to be barren. The original commission to man was to **"be fruitful**

and multiply" (Genesis 1:28). Of course, there are those who are barren in the natural but have many spiritual children, just as we read in Isaiah 54. There are also those who are celibates for the kingdom, such as Paul, and have many spiritual children. However, no one should be without spiritual children. So how do we reproduce spiritually? We do this with our words.

Just as the Lord explained in the Parable of the Sower that the seed was the Word of God, words are seeds. Words will spring up and bear fruit. As we are told in Proverbs 13:14, **"The teaching of the wise is a fountain of life…"** In Proverbs 18:21, we are told that **"Death and life are in the power of the tongue, and those who love it will eat its fruit."**

This leads us to a most important question. What kind of seeds are we sowing? Are we spreading life or death with our words? This of course is why the apostle tells us to gird our loins with truth. We want our words to be true above all things so that what we are reproducing with them is life. As the Lord said in Matthew 12:33-37:

> **"Either make the tree good and its fruit good, or make the tree bad and its fruit bad; for the tree is known by its fruit.**
>
> **"You brood of vipers, how can you, being evil, speak what is good? For the mouth speaks out of that which fills the heart.**
>
> **"The good man brings out of his good treasure what is good; and the evil man brings out of his evil treasure what is evil.**
>
> **"And I say to you, that every careless word that men shall speak, they shall render account for it in the day of judgment.**
>
> **"For by your words you shall be justified, and by your words you shall be condemned."**

If our words are to be truth and life, then we must wrap ourselves in the truth. We must love truth, pursue it, and cling to it as the greatest treasure. We must honor it by being devoted to speaking only the truth. Truth is the most basic and precious commodity that we have been entrusted with. In all things, it must be a most basic devotion in our life. This is why we see in II Thessalonians 2:10 that it is not just those who have truth, but those who have a **"love of the truth"** who will not be deceived in the last days. That is how we gird our loins with truth—we love truth enough to wrap ourselves in it continually.

Of course the truth we are talking about is God's Word. Just as a knight would arise and put on his armor each morning for the day's battles, we too need to arise first thing each day and wrap ourselves in God's Word. There are many other exhortations in Scripture to devote ourselves to God's Word the first thing each day. The priests were to wash themselves in the Laver the first thing each day, which represented the cleansing of the Word. The children of Israel were to gather the manna from heaven the first thing each morning, which represents the living Word of God. Here we see that we should put on our armor by girding ourselves with His truth. If we will spend just a short time in the Word the first thing each day, it will change our lives.

We should also be as concerned about spiritual barrenness as those in biblical times were about natural barrenness. We must protect our ability to reproduce, and we can only do this with a most basic devotion to truth, God's Word.

In the second part of Ephesians 6:14 we read:

and HAVING PUT ON THE BREASTPLATE OF RIGHTEOUSNESS,

The breastplate is protection for the vital organs—the heart and lungs. The heart pumps the blood, which is our life. The lungs are for breathing. The Hebrew word for breath is the same word used for spirit. Spiritually, our heart is the source of the life that flows through us, and our spiritual lungs represents our ability to interchange with the spiritual realm. Both of these are protected by putting on the breastplate of righteousness.

So what is the breastplate of righteousness? Righteousness is simply doing what is right in the sight of God. This is not something which we just casually try to do each day, but we must put it on as armor for our most vital spiritual organs. This is what we must put on to protect our hearts from the poison darts of the enemy who seeks to corrupt our hearts, or puncture our spiritual lungs so we can no longer breathe in the realm of the Spirit.

Obviously, the stronger this piece of armor, the more protection we have. The strength of this piece of armor will be dependent on the strength of our devotion to doing what is right in the sight of God. This is something the Scripture teaches which must be nurtured in our lives.

We also know that the spiritual armor given to us is for the places where the enemy is going to try to hit us. We can be sure he will continually try to penetrate our breastplate. If it is thin, he will get through. How strong is our devotion to doing what is right in the sight of God? That is precisely how strong our protection is for our most vital spiritual organs.

Because Isaiah 64:6 states, **"But we are all like an unclean thing, and all our righteousness are like filthy rags..."** and Romans 3:10, says, **"There is none righteous, not even one,"** some have been deceived into thinking that we can never be righteous, and therefore to even try is futile. This deception has caused many to stumble and depart from the grace of God, as the Scriptures also warned would happen. It is true we do not have any righteousness in ourselves, but we must understand this armor is **"the whole armor of God."** We are to put on His righteousness, not our own. This is a devotion to what He thinks is right, not what we think is right. What we tend to think is right is usually the equivalent of **"filthy rags."**

It is true that our righteousness is in God, acquired by faith in Him and His righteousness. But the Scriptures are clear that if we have true faith in Him we will abide in Him, and become like Him. We understand that regardless of how righteous we become in our actions, it is only because of His grace. If we are walking in the true grace of God, we will become righteous in our actions and in our hearts.

It is crucial that the confusion about righteousness be cleared up because this is the armor which protects our most vital organs. The following are just a few of the literally hundreds of Scriptures that testify and teach concerning the righteousness we are to walk in:

> **Thy throne, O God, is forever and ever; a scepter of uprightness is the scepter of Thy kingdom.**
>
> **You have loved righteousness and hated wickedness; therefore God, Thy God, has anointed Thee with the oil of joy above Thy fellows (Psalms 45:6-7).**

This of course was written about the Lord Jesus, to whose image we are to be conformed. If this is taking place, we should grow in our love of righteousness and our hatred of wickedness. If we are not growing in these, then somehow we have been diverted from the path of life. Likewise, consider the following verses from both the Old and New Testaments:

> **The righteousness of the blameless will smooth his way, but the wicked will fall by his own wickedness.**
>
> **The righteousness of the upright will deliver them, but the treacherous will be caught by their own greed (Proverbs 11:5-6).**
>
> **He who is steadfast in righteousness will attain to life, and he who pursues evil will bring about his own death.**
>
> **The perverse in heart are an abomination to the Lord, but the blameless in their walk are His delight (Proverbs 11:19-20).**
>
> **In the way of righteousness is life, and in its pathway there is no death (Proverbs 12:28).**
>
> **"Blessed are those who hunger and thirst for righteousness, for they shall be satisfied" (Matthew 5:6).**

"For I say to you that unless your righteousness surpasses that of the scribes and Pharisees, you shall not enter the kingdom of heaven" (Matthew 5:20).

Of course, the only way that our righteousness could exceed the righteousness of the scribes and Pharisees is for us to take on the righteousness of Christ. And if we have taken on His righteousness it will be evident, as we see in the following verses:

But now apart from the Law the righteousness of God has been manifested, being witnessed by the Law and the Prophets,

even the righteousness of God through faith in Jesus Christ for all those who believe; for there is no distinction;

for all have sinned and fall short of the glory of God,

being justified as a gift by His grace through the redemption which is in Christ Jesus (Romans 3:21-24).

He made Him who knew no sin to be sin on our behalf, that we might become the righteousness of God in Him (II Corinthians 5:21).

And this I pray, that your love may abound still more and more in real knowledge and all discernment,

so that you may approve the things that are excellent, in order to be sincere and blameless until the day of Christ;

having been filled with the fruit of righteousness which comes through Jesus Christ, to the glory and praise of God (Philippians 1:9-11).

For the love of money is a root of all sorts of evil, and some by longing for it have wandered away from the faith and pierced themselves with many a pang.

But flee from these things, you man of God, and pursue righteousness, godliness, faith, love, perseverance and gentleness (I Timothy 6:10-11).

All Scripture is inspired by God and profitable for teaching, for reproof, for correction, for training in righteousness;

so that the man of God may be adequate, equipped for every good work (II Timothy 3:16-17).

It is obvious in these Scriptures that when we take on the righteousness of Christ, we become the righteousness of Christ. One purpose for the Scriptures is for our training in righteousness.

This is obviously not just a one-time event when we get up and put on the righteousness of God, but it is a life pursuit. It is the result of a "hungering and thirsting" for righteousness. It should be a basic devotion of our lives to do what is right in the sight of God, to grow in our love of what is right in His sight, and to loathe what is wrong in His sight.

It is sometimes a struggle to hate the evil as the Lord does, but love those who are trapped in it. This comes with maturity. We must grow in the truth that we are putting on the righteousness of God, not our own, and that we would be just as evil as others if it were not for His grace. This is why we must also keep in mind the truth that **"God is opposed to the proud, but gives grace to the humble" (James 4:6).** It is terribly arrogant to think that we are better than others because we have more grace, and it can ultimately cost us our grace.

The devil will try to place stumbling blocks before us in our pursuit of every truth, but we must learn to step over them and keep going. The truth of the next verse is crucial if we are to do this:

"But seek first His kingdom and His righteousness, and all these things shall be added to you" (Matthew 6:33).

If we just seek the kingdom we will be imbalanced, and will ultimately totter in our walk. If we just seek His righteousness, we will likewise be imbalanced and ultimately totter. We must seek both His kingdom and His righteousness together if we are to have a balanced walk on the path of life which enables Him to add **"all these things"** to us. This is emphasized in one of the great New Testament verses, Romans 14:17:

for the kingdom of God is not eating and drinking, but righteousness and peace and joy in the Holy Spirit.

We see here that walking in the kingdom begins with righteousness. If we walk uprightly before the Lord we will know His peace, which will then open us up to the greatest joy which can be experienced on this earth—a life in union with the King.

CHAPTER TWENTY-THREE

Good Shoes, Big Shield

We continue our study of the armor of God in Ephesians 6:15:

and having shod YOUR FEET WITH THE PREPARATION OF THE GOSPEL OF PEACE;

Walkers and hikers know the value of good shoes. We, too, must consider that there is a reason why our "walk with the Lord" is called a "walk." It is not a static life. It has a certain destination and things to accomplish along the way. It is a glorious life and the greatest adventure which we can have on the earth, but it is also intended to be hard and challenging. Just as the shoes we wear on any challenging hike will have a major effect on the hike, we must have good spiritual shoes if we are going to do well in our spiritual walk.

In this verse we see how our shoes are actually a part of our armor. Shoes protect our feet from the rough ground that we must walk on. If we did not have this protection, our feet would become so wounded they would soon hinder, or even stop our walk. Our spiritual shoes are intended to do the same—they are our protection against the hard and rough things that we encounter in this life.

Someone once said, "Life is hard and then you die." Of course death is a glorious graduation for Christians, so to us it is a good thing. Even so, it is true that life is hard. We are called to walk upon very hard ground. As we approach the end of this age, it will become even more difficult. That is why we must give careful attention to this part of our armor. We need the best shoes for the best walk, and the best shoes are **"the preparation of the gospel of peace."**

It is interesting that the apostle does not say our feet must be shod by the gospel of peace, but by **"preparation"** for it. There is the gospel, but at times Paul also talked about his gospel. This was his life message. It was this message that he was called to preach especially to the Gentiles. He had made his calling and election sure by years of focused preparation. Of course few are called to have an extraordinary ministry like Paul's, but each one of us are called to have our own life message—a unique presentation of the gospel which is from our own experience in life and that prepared us for our purpose.

This in no way implies that we are to change the doctrine or basic message of the gospel. Neither is it a matter of personally interpreting either doctrine or prophecy. It is having living waters coming from our innermost being. It is the same thing Jesus commended Peter for when he declared Him to be the Christ. Peter had not just received this from other men's opinions, but he had received it straight from the Father himself.

Remember the story of the seven Jewish exorcists who tried to cast out demons by **"Jesus whom Paul preaches?" (Acts 19:13)** The demons were not impressed. Knowing someone who knows the Lord does not give us any authority. None of us will be saved because we believe in the Jesus that our parents know, or our pastor knows—He has to be our Jesus! This is what it means to have a personal gospel—it is the same message to all, but it has become personal to us. You can teach a parrot to say the words, but it will not have any power unless it comes from a heart which comprehends. People can be like parrots too, but their message will not be living unless it comes from their own hearts.

One of my favorite evangelists is Nicky Cruz. A couple of years ago I was with him in a meeting when he presented the gospel message which I know he has shared many thousands of times. However, it was as fresh and he was as enthusiastic about it as if he were sharing it for the first time. His passion for the simple gospel message of the grace of God to forgive sins is the result of his own personal salvation from such a depth of sin. You immediately know as he shares that this is not just a teaching about the grace of God, it is a living demonstration of the grace of God. Nicky has never lost touch with what a sinner he was, and how much love and grace God had for him to pluck him out of that sin.

What is your life message? What touches your heart the most about the gospel? Even though Paul preached **"the whole message of this life" (Acts 5:20),** it is obvious he had a special purpose in establishing the grace of God and His mercy toward the Gentiles. For Peter, it was that Jesus was the fulfillment of the hope of the Jews for their Messiah. For you, it may be reaching a certain city or a specific nation or people group.

The gospel message itself is so wonderful that it should always touch the very depths of our being. I have watched many Christians, regardless of how mature they are, be inspired again by the salvation of a single person. Indeed, even the angels in heaven rejoice at just one sinner who repents. We must never lose touch with the awesome grace and glory of God which is revealed through the gospel. And we should wrap this message around our walk with Christ like we put on our shoes and tie them securely. This message will protect us from the hardships of this life like nothing else can.

We, too, must be able to convey **"the whole message of this life."** However, it is obvious that all the messengers in Scripture and history also had a unique presentation of the gospel which made it *their* gospel. Again, what is your life message? Be free to be unique. If you are going to have a successful walk, you need good shoes. If you want a great walk, you need great shoes. Take the time to make yours the best shoes. Be free to be unique because your shoes must fit you, not someone else.

In Ephesians 6:16 we read:

in addition to all, taking up the shield of faith with which you will be able to extinguish all the flaming missiles of the evil one.

There are many aspects of faith. We enter into salvation by faith, and it is accounted to us as righteousness. Faith releases the power of God in our lives to do miracles—we even prophesy according to our faith. In the Scripture above, we see that faith is also the shield which will extinguish the flaming arrows of the enemy. This is truly an important use of our faith, but it seems that very few understand it, and fewer still use it this way.

There was a period of several years that whenever I prayed for someone I would see his or her spiritual armor. I could see the condition that it was in, and how it was worn. Everyone I prayed for had a shield of faith, but each was of a different size and condition. Many were so tiny that I did not think the shields would be useful at all. Others just kind of dragged their shield behind them instead of holding it up in front to protect them as they walked. These people were all wounded, and it was easy to see why.

If a soldier is marching toward you with his shield held rightly, it will almost certainly be the most prominent thing you see about him. If it is clean and shiny, it will be even more so. Can this be said of us? When others look at you, is your faith that prominent?

Our shield of faith is also what extinguishes any arrow the enemy fires at us. If we are constantly getting hurt and wounded, it is almost certainly because we are not carrying our faith right. Faith is basically seeing Jesus and knowing where He sits above all rule, authority, and power. If we know this, then it is impossible for the enemy to get a shot in while the Lord is not looking. Therefore, all of the trials which come our way are for a purpose—our maturity. We should therefore embrace the trials as opportunities. In this way, each trial the enemy flings at us will actually cause our faith to grow so it becomes even more difficult for him to wound us.

A skillful warrior in biblical times used his shield effectively regardless of which direction the attack was coming. A warrior who rigidly walked with his shield in one place would become an easy target for someone who shot at him from an unexpected direction. We, too, must learn to be flexible with our faith. There is faith for salvation and faith for healing. There is faith for authority over demons, and there is faith to bring in God's provision. There is faith for our children, churches, cities, and faith for our country, to see God move in all of them.

So if our faith is going to be useful for these, we must see them with trust in God and anticipation of His victory, not with doubt, regardless of what problems arise. The key is to keep our shields up, regardless of what disappointments may come. There are times when things will happen which could be very disappointing. However, to become disappointed is to drop our shield of faith. When arrows start coming, it is not the time to drop our shields, but to raise them up with even more resolve. The arrows will come, and should never discourage us, but it should cause us to grip our faith even tighter, and hold it up with even greater vigilance.

Are you now dragging your faith when it comes to your church, to your children, or your own calling and purpose in the Lord? Pick up your shield! Shine it. Determine that you are going to grow your shield until you are completely protected from the darts of the enemy, and even keep growing it until it is large enough to protect others as well.

CHAPTER TWENTY-FOUR

The Head
and the Hand

We continue our study of the armor of God in Ephesians 6:17:

And take THE HELMET OF SALVATION...

The helmet protects the head or the mind. If salvation is working in our lives, then our minds will be renewed. We will not continue to think the way that we did or the way the world does. If there is not a substantial difference between the way we think and those who do not know Christ, then we have somehow aborted the crucial process of having our minds renewed.

Even when our minds have been renewed, they need protection. This is what the helmet of salvation is for. It is the salvation that we have received that protects our minds. Salvation is so profound, such a dramatic contrast to our former life and way of thinking, that from the time we are born again the cross should be the one thing that determines what we allow in our minds or not.

Silver speaks of redemption in Scripture. The Israelites had to pay a half shekel of silver for their redemption (see Exodus 30:15). Also, the price given for Jesus was paid in silver. It is noteworthy that the acacia wood posts which held up the white linen fabric, enclosing the Outer Court of the Tabernacle, had silver bases and silver caps. The white linen represented God's righteousness, and the acacia wood pillars were a prophetic picture of how those who were called to uphold God's righteousness stood on redemption, and their heads were covered with redemption.

Many wrongly think that because they have their standing on the redemption of the cross, it does not matter what they do or think. However, if we are truly standing on the redemption of the cross so as to uphold the righteousness of God, it will cover our minds as well, and will be demonstrated by how we think. As we are told in Proverbs 23:7, **"For as he thinks within himself, so he is."**

If we are going to wear the whole armor of God, the helmet is one of the crucial pieces. Do we protect our minds with the salvation of God? Do we allow the cross to determine what we read, watch on television, or even the conversations we listen to? As we are told in Galatians 6:7-8:

> **Do not be deceived, God is not mocked; for whatever a man sows, this he will also reap.**
>
> **For the one who sows to his own flesh shall from the flesh reap corruption, but the one who sows to the Spirit shall from the Spirit reap eternal life.**

What are we sowing into our minds? This is why the apostle also stated in Philippians 4:8:

> **Finally, brethren, whatever is true, whatever is honorable, whatever is right, whatever is pure, whatever is lovely, whatever is of good repute, if there is any excellence and if anything worthy of praise, let your mind dwell on these things.**

Where do our minds dwell most of the time? What kind of seeds do we allow to be sown into them? What kind of television programs do we watch? What kind of books or magazines do we read? If we are going to have the mind of Christ, we must protect ourselves from the evil seeds that the devil and the world would try to sow into us. We must also give ourselves to sowing the good seed of the Word of God into our minds.

In the second half of Ephesians 6:17, we read that we must also take up **"...the sword of the Spirit, which is the word of God."** The sword is part of the armor and is used for protection, but it is also the only offensive weapon we have been given. First let us consider how it is used defensively.

I have a friend, Dr. John Chacha, who grew up in one of the poorest villages in Africa. When he went to school, his teachers used to tell him that it was useless for him to seek an education, since he was doomed to a life of poverty from which he could never escape. Fortunately, he continued going to school even though he believed his teachers—the primary authority figures in his life. Then he became a Christian and started reading the Bible. He read that if he had faith in God he could do anything. He determined to believe the Word of God over what he had been told by his teachers. When he heard about America, he started believing he could go to America and begin a successful ministry there.

When a way was provided for him to go to America, he did not hesitate. He arrived with $85 in his pocket, rejoicing that he had so much to sow as seed for his new ministry, and he gave it all away. In a short time Dr. Chacha had a thriving ministry in America, but his heart was still for the multitudes in Africa. He wanted to see them break free of the devil's curse over them which had tried to doom his own life. He started going back to Africa where he has now helped to start nearly five hundred Bible schools. Already thousands who have been released into ministry all over the continent, are carrying the Word of God to some of the world's poorest people, setting them free.

As a defensive weapon, the sword of the Spirit is especially used to block the sword of the devil, which of course is the word of the devil. The devil repeatedly prophesied over Dr. Chacha that he could never escape the poverty of his little village in Africa. As soon as the sword of the Spirit was put in his hand, he used it to block those negative prophecies by simply determining to believe the Word of God above anything else. Dr. Chacha continues to see many miracles because he simply believes the Word of God over anything else that he hears.

The sword of the Spirit can block any word the devil sends at us. All we have to do is use it. Is that not what Jesus did when the devil tempted Him? Repeatedly He said, **"It is written!"** If the Word Himself would so use the written word, how much more should we? What negative words have been spoken over you? Words like: "You'll never be a success. Your marriage will fail. You're going to die of cancer like your parent," etc. You need to immediately take up the sword of the Spirit against those swords of the devil and drive them back. They will only be true prophecies if you do not resist them.

Now let's talk about how we use the sword of the Spirit offensively. II Corinthians 10:4-5 says:

> **for the weapons of our warfare are not of the flesh, but divinely powerful for the destruction of fortresses.**
>
> **We are destroying speculations and every lofty thing raised up against the knowledge of God, and we are taking every thought captive to the obedience of Christ.**

The devil erects fortresses of deception to keep people in bondage with his negative words. He uses fear to bind people the way the Lord uses faith to set them free. Words are without question the most powerful force in the world. The Word of God has the power of God behind it. This is why statements that were spoken under the anointing of the Spirit have changed history more than armies ever could.

Leo Tolstoy, possibly the greatest novelist of all time, once said, "Prophecy is like a fire that is lit in a dry wood. It will burn and burn and burn until all of the wood, hay, and stubble is consumed." Tolstoy used the destruction of slavery as an example of this. When righteous men and women spoke under the anointing that slavery was wrong, a fire began to burn all over the world. Within decades an institution which had existed all over the world since the beginning of recorded history ceased to exist on the earth, except in a few scattered, remote places.

During the Civil War, when Abraham Lincoln met Harriet Beecher Stowe, who had written the book, *Uncle Tom's Cabin,* he said to her, "So you're the little lady who started this great war!" Words, spoken or written under the anointing of God, have a power like none other on earth. We have been entrusted with this power and must learn to use it until every evil stronghold has been destroyed.

Of course the ultimate stronghold of the devil over the earth will be broken by the sword which comes from the Lord's own mouth when He returns. However, we are not supposed to wait until then to use what He has entrusted to us. What are the evil strongholds in your family? Ask the Lord to give you the anointed words to speak over your family. Find the Scriptures that address the problem and begin to speak them, pray them, and believe them.

Are there evil strongholds at the office or warehouse where you work? Is there slander, backbiting, bitterness, or stealing? As Christians we should take it as a personal insult from the devil when he does this kind of thing in our spiritual domain, and we should go on the offensive against him. Start speaking the Word of God over your fellow employees.

When you do this, you do not need to tell others what you're doing. If there is stealing going on, determine first that this evil will not conquer you, and resolve to always walk in the highest standards of honesty and integrity. Determine that walking in truth and the honor befitting of a child of the King is more important than any promotion or advantage a little deception may give you. When you see others being taken over by this spirit of cheating or stealing, ask the Lord to give you words to speak over them about how they are going to be standards of integrity and honor, etc. You will see changes. Sometimes it takes a while to tear down especially thick strongholds, but they will come down.

These are just a couple of brief examples of how we must learn to use the sword of the Spirit. Two of my most recent books, *Breaking the Power of Evil,* and *Overcoming Evil in*

the Last Days, address this subject in a lot more depth and scope. I have received a lot of responses from people who think these are the two most powerful books I have yet written. I appreciate the encouragement, but what encourages me even more is to hear of the strongholds the devil has had in people's lives being destroyed. We must get free, we must set all of our brothers and sisters in Christ free, and then we must go after every evil stronghold which the devil has erected to keep mankind in bondage. Let us be found so doing when the Lord returns. It is time to start using the sword which has been given to us!

CHAPTER TWENTY-FIVE

The Most
Powerful Weapon

Before going on to our next verse in this study, it would be appropriate to look briefly at the way some of the issues concerning spiritual warfare and the armor of God are being widely misunderstood. I personally did not feel these issues were so crucial until I had the visions that I wrote about in **The Final Quest** where I saw the army of God. In one of those visions, only a few members of this army had on their armor and many of them only had on a piece or two. The result was they were easily defeated by the enemy. Since then, I have seen the truth of this and the resulting devastation in many lives.

I have run into an amazing number of believers who have neglected not only the armor of God, but have formulated doctrines which they believe, and in some cases even teach, saying those who have enough faith, do not need this armor. Some have even declared that those who take on the armor of God are immature in their faith. Certainly faith is a shield, and it may seem if we have a big enough shield we would not need any other armor. However, taking on the **"full armor of God"** must be important, or the Lord would not have emphasized this. The fact is that we are still immature and foolish if we are so easily swayed by such teachings that are in clear contradiction to the Scriptures. Those who are so easily fooled by such unbiblical teaching inevitably become the spiritual casualties like those who are strewn across the landscape of Christianity at this time.

One of the reasons for this in-depth, verse by verse study of Ephesians is to try and stimulate a deeper devotion to the Scriptures and a desire to sink our roots deeper and deeper into sound, biblical doctrine. A primary root of the meltdown of morality, light, and power within the church has been a tendency throughout the body of Christ to drift from the clear mandates of Scripture and start holding to beliefs which are based more on someone's opinions. These often come in the cloak of a super-spiritual idealism, which in itself should set off alarms in us.

I have also heard other believers say that they do not need to emphasize the armor of God because God is their Shepherd and He will protect them. God does protect us—with the armor He provided for us! Of course, He protects us much more than that too, but to disregard such clear biblical instructions is a little more than just foolishness—it is a symptom of the same kind of rebellion which led to the first sin in the garden. Idealism is a form of rebellion. Regardless of how subtle it may be, it is actually saying that we know better than God, or have a higher wisdom than His Word. As incredible as this may seem, our fallen nature will continually try to challenge God in this way.

We can absolutely count on the protection of God from any power of the evil one as long as we walk in obedience. Some think this puts the responsibility for protection back on themselves and that is true, to a degree. Every promise of God has conditions. We see repeatedly in the Old Testament that the Lord promised Israel great blessing, prosperity, and protection, as long as they served Him according to His statutes. He then repeatedly warned them of what would happen if they failed to keep their part of the covenant. We also see this repeated in the New Testament. If we put on the armor which God has provided for us, we can resist the devil and quench the fiery darts he throws at us. If we do not put on the armor, we can count on those shots hitting us.

The foolish believers who suffer wounding by the devil because of their own idealism or rebellion will almost inevitably blame God, the church, or almost anyone for it but themselves. In Romans 1:5 and 16:26, we see the phrase **"obedience of faith."** True faith is fundamentally a commitment to obey God's instructions. Faith which is evidenced by obedience is a shield and none of the fiery darts the enemy sends will be able to penetrate it.

The armor is crucial or it would not have been given to us. However, greater than the entire armor is our access to come boldly before the throne of God to seek the grace we need. This is not only the ultimate privilege, it is also the ultimate responsibility as the priests we are all called to be in the New Covenant.

As we see in our verse for this chapter, after Paul highlights the importance of each piece of the armor of God, he then directs us to use the greatest weapon of all—prayer! This we read in Ephesians 6:18:

> **With all prayer and petition pray at all times in the Spirit, and with this in view, be on the alert with all perseverance and petition for all the saints.**

As we covered previously, the main reason we must ask, even though the Lord already knows what we need, is found in Psalm 115:16: **"The heavens are the heavens of the Lord, but the earth He has given to the sons of men."** The Lord has delegated His authority on the earth to men. He, therefore, will not intervene on the earth unless we ask Him. The reverse is one of the greatest and most important truths of all—if we ask Him, He will intervene on our behalf! God answers prayer. There is no greater weapon that we could ever have than our ability to go before the very throne of God anytime we want and find the grace we need.

Some of the great books of our time, and all time, have been written on this subject—prayer. However, many Christians become frustrated in their prayer life and drift from using this most powerful weapon, and greatest privilege. Remember that one of the enemy's most basic strategies against the church is to "wear out the saints." Believe it or not, one of the enemy's main strategies to keep you from praying is to wear you out in prayer by having you pray too much. The devil will try to make you feel guilty because you are not praying at least an hour each day, or even more, when the Lord may have only called you to spend five minutes in prayer each day. Let me explain.

First, I think it is certainly noble to want to pray for an hour each day, and I will even agree this would be good for every believer. However, if you try to get there too fast you will probably fail, and may even drift from prayer altogether. If you will start with trying to be faithful to pray just five minutes each day, you will soon start to love prayer. Then you will find yourself automatically going ten minutes, and then twenty... Soon you will be so addicted to prayer and the presence of the Lord that your whole life will begin to revolve around trying to find time to get away and pray.

It is also good to pray for specific things. You may even want to keep a prayer journal of the things which you are praying for, and leave room for logging when the prayers are answered. The encouragement of this will help you greatly. If you are having any kind of trouble with prayer, ask the Holy Spirit to help you pray (which is one of His jobs), and you will be amazed at how He will do this.

We must keep in mind that even though prayer is a responsibility given to every priest, which we all are called to be, it is not a burden, but a privilege. If you are watching the clock and can't wait to get it over with, back off! You are trying to do too much, too fast. No one is ever glad when their conversation is over with the one they love. Somehow your conversation has turned into a religious ritual if you can't wait for the time to be up. Return to your first love. Do not give up on prayer, but pray out of love, taking small but steady steps toward maturity in it.

Above all things we must keep in mind that prayer itself is not the goal—but rather a part of seeing His kingdom come and His will being done on the earth. Prayer is a means to draw near to Him. Our goal should be to become so unified with Him that we are always praying according to His will. Then we know our prayers will be answered. This takes maturity, but in all things we should be growing and maturing. If our prayer life is not maturing, then we are almost certainly caught in a dead religious exercise at best. Our goal should be to grow in our relationship with the Lord and our faith in Him, until all of our prayers are answered.

Prayer is our most powerful weapon because prayer can move God. Are your prayers moving Him? If not, find the answer to this ultimate question. Nothing may change your life more.

From my studies of history, it was apparent that every great man or woman of God who had a true impact on their generation was profoundly devoted to prayer. With most, it was the central devotion of their life. In contrast to this, recent studies of the American church revealed that the average pastor spends less than five minutes a day in prayer. This is obviously the reason for much of the weakness and lukewarmness of so many churches today. If this just doubled and every pastor in America began to spend just ten minutes a day in prayer, we would probably see a radical change in American Christianity. When prayer again takes its rightful place in the life of the body of Christ, we will become an irresistible force.

There are numerous great books on prayer available. I would encourage you to read a book on prayer regularly. The Lord sent fire from heaven to ignite the fire on the altar of burnt offering, but then commanded the priests to keep it going. Likewise, when He ignites a fire in our lives He expects us to keep it going. Get with other believers who are committed to prayer. Go to prayer meetings where there is a true fire burning, and determine that you are going to be one who adds to the fire. The main one who will benefit from this will be you and the ones you love.

CHAPTER TWENTY-SIX

The Watchman

In this chapter, I want to continue our consideration of Ephesians 6:18:

> **With all prayer and petition pray at all times in the Spirit, and with this in view, be on the alert with all perseverance and petition for all the saints.**

Think for one moment how radically our lives would be transformed if all the time and energy we wasted on vain imaginations was turned into prayer? This is what the apostle is appealing for in this verse, and it should be a primary goal of every believer to be able to pray in the Spirit at all times.

And Paul goes on to say, **"with this in view, be on the alert with all perseverance."** One of the designations of a prophet in the Old Testament was **"watchman."** It was the watchman's job to be awake and discerning. It was also the job of the watchman to pray, as we see in Scriptures such as Isaiah 62:6-7:

> **On your walls, O Jerusalem, I have appointed watchmen; all day and all night they will never keep silent. You who remind the LORD, take no rest for yourselves;**

> **And give Him no rest until He establishes and makes Jerusalem a praise in the earth.**

When I was in the military, we had military police and others whose job it was to be on guard at all times. However, everyone had to stand watch at appointed times, regardless of what his job was. Everyone was trained to stand watch, and knew that one of the worst offenses was to sleep while on watch. The lives of many people depended on the watchmen staying awake. In times of war, a watchman who slept while on duty could jeopardize the entire nation. Therefore, the penalty for such neglect was most severe. The body of Christ is likewise paying a very high price and suffering many unnecessary defeats, because many of its watchmen are sleeping.

There are many other tragedies caused simply by posting watchmen, without properly equipping them. During the inquiry into the sinking of the Titanic, it was discovered that the watchmen who had been posted that tragic night when it struck the iceberg, did not even have binoculars. If the watchmen had been given these, they would have easily seen the iceberg in time to avoid it. The very watchmen who were on duty that night had made written requests for binoculars and had been ignored. The inquiry concluded that the Titanic was lost, and many passengers died, for the lack of a $10 pair of binoculars.

It was because of my conviction concerning this tragedy, that I wrote a booklet in 1987 entitled, *The Titanic and the Stock Market,* which caused me to be devoted to providing a place where prophetic people could be equipped. Since then, I have documented numerous cases of devastating spiritual attacks being suffered by churches and ministries who neglected clear prophetic warnings. If we do not wake up to the importance of the watchman ministry by recognizing, posting, equipping, and listening to them, the unnecessary tragedies will continue.

There are some whose calling is to be watchmen on the walls of their church, ministry, or city. However, this is something every believer should be trained in, and able to stand watch at any time. Regardless of whether this is our primary calling in the Lord, or whether we are just called on to do it during rotations, it should be something we take with the utmost seriousness. We will not know until eternity how many of the devil's attacks worked because of those who were called to watch were sleeping.

Of course, God never sleeps, but the mature believer understands delegated authority—God has delegated authority to us, and He will not intervene unless asked. The devil cannot get a shot in while God is not looking, but God will let him hit us if we are being irresponsible. This is one of the ways the Lord matures us so He can trust us with more authority.

Because ministries have spheres of authority, to be an effective watchman we must know our realm of authority. If an infantryman in the army is called on to guard a skirmish line in the trenches, but he keeps trying to see what is going on in the whole war, the enemy could sneak up on him. I appreciate the United States military doctrine where they try to keep all of their men generally informed as to what is happening, but it is not good for a corporal to be overly concerned about the big picture strategy of the war. Neither should a general spend his precious time at the guard post on a skirmish line.

If the Lord has made us a watchman for a home group, we need to take this most seriously. It is good to have a general picture of what is going on throughout the church, and to pray for other things as well, but we must focus on our realm of authority if we are going to be properly on the alert for it. Those who are faithful on one level will probably get promoted to larger realms of authority. There is a point at which you are called to be a watchman for a movement or even the whole church. However, at this point you really cannot spend a lot of time praying for individuals without being kept from your main purpose.

In the verse we have been studying, Paul exhorts us to pray at all times for all of the saints. We should pray for the whole army of God, and not just for our little platoon or company. We do all have some responsibility for the whole, and this is an appropriate prayer for all believers.

We should also consider that our prayers ought to be mostly for people, not just places, events, etc. We must never forget that one person in unity with God is the most powerful force on the earth. Therefore, we should always keep our prayers and our ministry focused on people.

PART VIII

The Foundation
of Eternal Life

Paul's Last Charge
to the Glorious Church

CHAPTER TWENTY-SEVEN

Ambassador in Chains

In the verse we addressed in the last chapter, Paul encourages believers to pray for the purposes of God, and one another. In Ephesians 6:19-20, he asks for prayer for himself:

and pray on my behalf, that utterance may be given to me in the opening of my mouth, to make known with boldness the mystery of the gospel,

for which I am an ambassador in chains; that in proclaiming it I may speak boldly, as I ought to speak.

It is the setting which makes this one of the most remarkable verses in the entire Epistle. Paul was in prison when he wrote this letter. His execution was likely to come soon. You would think he would have desperately asked the church to pray for his release in the very first sentence of this Epistle, but he never asks for this. Asking for prayer at all for himself seems like it was an afterthought. Then, what he asks for is not freedom for himself or anything for himself, but rather for the message, the gospel, to go forth unhindered. This is unquestionably the letter of a man who had truly emptied himself of anything but a desire to have the glory of his God made known.

One would think the Lord would be so moved by compassion for this most faithful servant as to send legions of angels to set him free. There is no question of the Lord's favor for one who truly was **"not in the least inferior to the most eminent apostles" (II Corinthians 11:5).** However, He showed His favor by letting this great apostle remain in prison, so he could write even more letters which would help set the course of history, and then finish his course with martyrdom.

It is also a truly remarkable thing that the King of kings would even allow the imprisonment of one of His greatest ambassadors, and possibly the greatest messenger of freedom to ever walk the earth. However, He allowed this because within it there is another great message—those who are truly free can never be imprisoned. Neither is there a jail on earth which can restrain the Word of God. This is possibly the reason some of the most powerful messages of freedom throughout history have been penned by those who were in prison.

Paul is certainly the greatest of these messengers of freedom. His words from prison have set countless people free from every form of bondage. His story is one of the most inspiring stories of all of the great men and women who have walked with God. His letters form the heart of the New Testament, and have possibly been used to change the world more than any words ever written.

Not only did Paul write the bulk of these Epistles from prison, but he didn't even have a laptop! No email, no fax machine—not even a phone! He did not have a worldwide television ministry, or even a mailing list for getting the word out. Yet, there almost certainly have never been any words penned in a human language which have been distributed more widely, or read and studied more thoroughly.

I am not belittling the incredible advantages that we have today with modern technology. Much is being accomplished which we should truly appreciate. However, the Word of God cannot be shackled or limited by technology or the lack of it— neither are the messengers of the Word of God. We should use what advantages we have been blessed with, but if we lose them all, and are even imprisoned, it will not restrain the Holy Spirit in any way from continuing to use us, possibly even in a greater way. In fact, it would probably even make the work of the Holy Spirit more evident.

I hear almost daily the laments of people who say, if they just did not have to work so much they could do more ministry. I hear ministries constantly lamenting if they just had more money, or more equipment, they could do so much more for the gospel. There is a higher faith, one which can accomplish far more regardless of the circumstances or the limitations.

This is not to imply that we should not seek situations and aids which will help us in the promulgation of the gospel, but this needs to come from a foundation of having the faith to see the most remarkable results from any little thing that God puts in our hands. To paraphrase what the Lord told Moses when he began to lament about his limitations, "What is that in your hand? A staff? Fine. That's all you'll need." How much glory would the Lord have received if Moses had a large army of his own, which he could take with him to set the Israelites free? If we really want the Lord to get the glory, we need to realize that He still likes to use the weak, the foolish, or we might say, "the limited" to show His unlimited power.

As we read in the next verses, Ephesians 6:21-22:

But that you also may know about my circumstances, how I am doing, Tychicus, the beloved brother and faithful minister in the Lord, will make everything known to you.

I have sent him to you for this very purpose, so that you may know about us, and that he may comfort your hearts.

What were Paul's circumstances? And how was he doing in his circumstances? As stated, he was in prison—his execution likely. In spite of this, instead of asking for desperate prayer or other help, he was more concerned for the Ephesian believers, that they would not be discouraged. So he sends his faithful friend Tychicus to encourage them. It seems that if anyone needed encouragement it would have been Paul! Not so! Paul was much more concerned for the Lord's children, and seemed oblivious to his own needs.

In Philippians 4:11-13, Paul gives us insight into his remarkable devotion which will forever make him one of the great examples of a faithful minister of the gospel:

Not that I speak from want, for I have learned to be content in whatever circumstances I am.

I know how to get along with humble means, and I also know how to live in prosperity; in any and every circumstance I have learned the secret of being filled and going hungry, both of having abundance and suffering need.

I can do all things through Him who strengthens me.

He certainly proved he lived this way by his words from prison. He saw every trial as an opportunity to see His Lord do wonders. When God did not do a miracle for him, Paul resolved that the Lord wanted him to grow in faith and patience—so he cheerfully embraced every condition that he was put in. As he wrote in I Timothy 6:8-12 to one of his favorite sons in the Lord:

If we have food and covering, with these we shall be content.

But those who want to get rich fall into temptation and a snare and many foolish and harmful desires which plunge men into ruin and destruction.

For the love of money is a root of all sorts of evil, and some by longing for it have wandered away from the faith and pierced themselves with many a pang.

But flee from these things, you man of God; and pursue righteousness, godliness, faith, love, perseverance and gentleness.

Fight the good fight of faith; take hold of the eternal life to which you were called, and you made the good confession in the presence of many witnesses.

Those who learn to live by this uncommon devotion to the Lord will likewise accomplish much on this earth for the kingdom, and will for eternity be among the most esteemed in the household of the King.

CHAPTER TWENTY-EIGHT

An Incorruptible Love

In the last two verses of our study of Ephesians 6:23-24, we come to the conclusion of Paul's great Epistle, and a remarkable summary of the entire message:

> **Peace be to the brethren, and love with faith, from God the Father and the Lord Jesus Christ.**

> **Grace be with all those who love our Lord Jesus Christ with a love incorruptible.**

This concluding statement to such an expansive vision summarizes the devotion that will enable us to walk in this ultimate purpose, which we have been given.

It begins with a blessing of peace. Paul himself was demonstrating the power of this peace in a most amazing way by being able to write such a letter in the midst of his own most trying circumstances. This is a basic secret of the power of the gospel itself. If we would abide in the peace of God during our trials, instead of worrying and fretting, we too would find in the midst of them an opportunity to minister that which would bring forth eternal fruit.

Next, Paul's blessing for the Ephesians is for them to have **"love with faith."** Faith without love can be bold and do exciting works, but not the works that will change anyone's life or bear eternal fruit. Likewise, love without faith can be an emotion that does not accomplish anything for the ones we claim to love.

I have been blessed with an abundance of some of the greatest friends I could have ever even hoped for. They are not only a constant joy to be with, they are exciting because of their unrelenting pursuit of the grace of God. Together they carry the bulk of the burdens in the ministry, and even to some degree in my personal life. However, occasionally someone will come who says they are sent specifically to be my friend, and tell me repeatedly how much they love me, but are much more of a drain and burden than the kind of addition that true love is supposed to be. With these, I believe they feel an emotion which they interpret to be love, but it really revolves around what I can do for them rather than what they can do for me as they claim.

This is easy to fall into at times, and I have probably done the same thing to others. However, my real concern is how we tend to treat the Lord this way. Does our love for Him really revolve around what He can do for us, rather than being a true love, always seeking to do for Him? When we are immature, it is understandable that our "love" is mostly selfish, just as an infant's attraction to its mother is mostly because of its own needs. However, true maturity is found in true love which is not self-seeking, but devoted to serving the one we love.

Paul is one of the great examples of true love found in the Scriptures. He is the one with the greatest burdens, actually in chains as a prisoner awaiting execution, and all he can think about is how to encourage the Lord's people. This is the kind of love with faith that he is trying to impart to the Ephesians, and it is the kind of love we should all pursue if we expect to be truly used for the gospel.

Then Paul prays the blessing of grace to those who love the Lord with an incorruptible love. This is the ultimate blessing that we could ever have. There is nothing in the universe more powerful than the grace of God, and there is nothing more valuable than an incorruptible love.

One of the best illustrations of the grace of God that I have ever heard came through a prophetic experience that a friend of mine named Bob Jones had. In this experience, he was caught up into another realm and saw the Lord. To his astonishment the Lord took him to a baseball game. In this game, the Lord's team was playing Satan's team. The score was tied and it was the bottom of the last inning, there were two outs, and the Lord's team was at bat.

A batter stepped up to the plate and his name was "Love." Satan wound up, threw the ball, and Love knocked it into the outfield for a base hit, because **"love never fails."** Then the next batter stepped up to the plate and his name was "Faith." He also knocks the first pitch into the outfield for a base hit, because "faith works with love."

Then a third batter stepped up to the plate and his name was "Godly Wisdom." Satan wound up and threw the first pitch, but Godly Wisdom looked it over and let it pass. It was ball one. Then Satan threw three more pitches and Godly Wisdom let them all pass, because "godly wisdom does not swing at Satan's pitches." He walked and the bases were loaded.

Then the Lord turned to Bob and said, "I have been saving My greatest player for this time," and "Grace" stepped up to the plate. Bob said he did not look like much, and Satan's whole team relaxed. Satan threw the ball and Bob said he had never seen one hit so hard. However, Satan's team was not worried because their center fielder, the prince of the air, did not let anything get by him. He went up for the ball and it went right through his glove, hit him in the head, and sent him crashing to the ground. The ball continued on over the fence for a grand slam. The Lord's team had won.

Then the Lord turned to Bob and said, "Do you know why Love, Faith, and Godly Wisdom could get on base, but they could not win the game? If your love, your faith, or your wisdom could win for you alone you would think you had done it. Your love, your faith, and your wisdom can only take you so far. It takes My grace to bring you home."

It is only by the grace of God that we have any love, faith, or wisdom. Even so, none of these alone can bring us the victory, but everything is dependent on God's grace. If we build our lives on the grace of God, then we will not just have love, we will have an **"incorruptible love."** Think about that—a love which will never compromise, never fall to the temptations of this world, but like that which is demonstrated by the apostle Paul, remain pure and undefiled until the end. Isn't that the ultimate vision, the ultimate purpose, which we are here to pursue? It is this **"incorruptible love"** which is the basis for an incorruptible life that will last forever. If we attain to this, then we will walk in all of the other extraordinary purposes which we have studied in the most remarkable Epistle of Paul to the Ephesians.

OTHER BOOKS BY RICK JOYNER

*To order any of these books, please call 1-800-542-0278
or order online at www.morningstarministries.org.*

MORE FROM MORNINGSTAR

**Call 1-800-542-0278 to request
a FREE MorningStar catalog
or find our online catalog at
www.morningstarministries.org**